To
Geoff & E
Merry Chri

Ben

22

**invite
PRESS**

WHAT
JESUS
EXPECTS
OF US

WHAT
JESUS
EXPECTS
OF US

SCOTT ENGLE

invite
PRESS

Plano, Texas

21 22 23 24 25 26 27 28 29 30 – 10 9 8 7 6 5 4 3 2 1
MANUFACTURED IN THE UNITED STATES OF AMERICA

Contents

Contents

Part IV: To Take Action

Part V: To Lead

Acknowledgments

First, I want to thank my wife Patti, my partner in love, life, and ministry. My work over the last twenty years would never have happened were it not for her encouragement and guiding wisdom. She will never really know what a blessing she is to me.

I also want to thank Len Wilson of Invite Resources and Nancy Kurkowski, a member of St. Andrew. Len's experience and talent has enabled us at St. Andrew to set up this publishing arm. Without it, there would be no book. And Nancy . . . well, she is the one who conceived this volume and then did the hard work of going through hundreds of studies I've written and pulling a selection of them together in this volume, editing and comparing them along the way. As I recall, even the title is Nancy's. Without her volunteering for this project, there would be no book. I could not have done it.

My special thanks also go to Rev. Robert Hasley and Rev. Arthur Jones. Robert has been an unflagging encourager of me and my ministry for the last two decades, even inviting me to take over the pulpit in one of our Sunday services. Arthur is a good friend and a gifted shepherd and preacher. It is his vision that is being realized in Invite Resources and he is only getting started. Robert and Arthur have always done all they can to help me continue in this, even as the years mounted.

Finally, my thanks go out to the entire St. Andrew family. So very many thoughtful, committed Christians and friends. I could never begin to list all those who have helped out over the years -- it is just too many. They have always encouraged me and let me know how God has used me and Patti to help them in their reading of Scripture and their walk with God. They are my brothers and sisters. I love them all.

Introduction

The apostle Paul once wrote a letter to circulate among the earliest house churches in western Asia Minor, imploring them "**to lead a life worthy of the calling** to which you have been called" (Ephesians 4:1). His challenge resonates just as strongly today.

But what does it mean to lead a worthy life?

It is a question being asked less and less often. Instead, I hear mostly about all the blessings that Jesus is going to pour out on us, and he does. We want Jesus to heal our wounds, cure our sicknesses, strengthen our marriages. We want Jesus to be our therapist, our life coach. But what if we could pray not just to receive blessings, but to understand what Jesus expects of us, and for the power to hear and to act? For Jesus charged us with doing more.

Jesus said that we are to "make disciples of all nations, baptizing them . . . teaching them to obey" (Matthew 28:19-20) and to be Jesus' "witnesses in Jerusalem, in all Judea and Samaria, and to the ends of the earth" (Acts 1:8). A worthy life is grounded in the love of Christ, and marked by humility, gentleness, and patience as we embrace our oneness in Christ (Ephesians 4:2-5). It is a life infused by a genuine love of others and of God, a love that is not sentimental but is lived out in our service, our worship, and our building up for his kingdom. Yes, all this is what Jesus expects of us and hopes for us.

This book offers a set of Bible studies to help us answer the question, "What does Jesus expect of us?" It assumes that Jesus is more than a divine vending machine—that with faith comes responsibility. Every chapter has a single purpose in mind: to open up the pages of Scripture so that you, the reader, might "have the power to comprehend, with all the saints [i.e., believers], what is the breadth and length and height and depth, and to know the love of Christ that surpasses knowledge, so that you may be filled with all the fullness of God" (Ephesians 3:18-19).

Let's say you undertake to read through the entire Bible in a year. What good will it do you if you don't connect some dots, grasp the larger story of

God's redemptive work, and generally comprehend what you are reading? These studies will help. Not only can you reflect on what Jesus expects of us all, you will begin to understand the biblical story and our shared faith in ways you may not have before. My suggestion is to read a chapter daily and then put the book away for a while. Come back later and read them again. This is how we learn . . . at least it is how I've learned and how I've heard God's Word as I never had before. Indeed, faith does seek understanding.

Scott L. Engle
Plano, Texas

PART I

TO GO ALL IN

If what we claim to be true about Jesus is actually true, then how can we hold anything back? If Jesus of Nazareth was resurrected and is the Word, who in the beginning was with God and is God (John 1:1), then, of course, he expects us to go all in: no half measures, no wait-and-see, no fence sitting. Nothing but full devotion to our Lord will do.

We have been called by him to be his disciples, his apprentices. Hence, we are to be more like Jesus every day, to be Christlike, manifested in the concrete acts of love we offer to God and to others. As Jesus' half-brother taught, "What good is it if we see someone hungry and offer them only a good word and not a good meal?" (See James 2:15-16.) We must commit ourselves to a lifetime of faithful worshipping, caring, learning, and serving. To go all in is nothing less than setting aside our selfish ambitions and putting the interests of others ahead of our own (Philippians 2:3-4). This must be our way 24/7, with nothing held back. And in this, we will find the joy and passion and fulfillment we each seek. We were made for this!

Chapter 1

Lukewarm about God?

Jeremiah 29:10–14

For thus says the LORD: Only when Babylon's seventy years are completed will I visit you, and I will fulfill to you my promise and bring you back to this place. For surely I know the plans I have for you, says the LORD, plans for your welfare and not for harm, to give you a future with hope. Then when you call upon me and come and pray to me, I will hear you. When you search for me, you will find me; if you seek me with all your heart, I will let you find me, says the LORD, and I will restore your fortunes and gather you from all the nations and all the places where I have driven you, says the LORD, and I will bring you back to the place from which I sent you into exile.

Revelation 3:14–22

And to the angel of the church in Laodicea write: The words of the Amen, the faithful and true witness, the origin of God's creation: "I know your works; you are neither cold nor hot. I wish that you were either cold or hot. So, because you are lukewarm, and neither cold nor hot, I am about to spit you out of my mouth. For you say, 'I am rich, I have prospered, and I need nothing.' You do not realize that you are wretched, pitiable, poor, blind, and naked. Therefore, I counsel you to buy from me gold refined by fire so that you may be rich; and white robes to clothe you and to keep the shame of your nakedness from being seen; and salve to anoint your eyes so that you may see. I reprove and discipline those whom I love. Be earnest, therefore, and repent. Listen! I am standing at the door, knocking; if you hear my voice and open the door, I will come in to you and eat with you, and you with me. To the one who conquers I will give a place with me on my throne, just as I myself conquered and sat down with my Father on his throne. Let anyone who has an ear listen to what the Spirit is saying to the churches."

Hot, Cold, or Lukewarm?

How would you characterize your own relationship with God?

This passage from Revelation hits my heart hard each time I read it. You see, I know that I spent much of my adult life as a Laodicean Christian.

1

I went to church much of the time, sang in the choir, and taught Sunday School now and then, but I was lukewarm. I would have told someone that I believed in Jesus and would have been able to spout some smart-sounding theology, but I was rather indifferent to the whole thing. I could take care of my own needs quite well, or so I thought. Sadly, I did not realize all this at the time. It is only by looking back from my new life in Christ that I can see my tepid faith for what it was.

When I read that Jesus wants to spit these wealthy, lukewarm Laodiceans out of his mouth, I take a big gulp and thank God that he grabbed me rather than tossed me.

Which Is It?

It is no surprise to us that Jesus would prefer the Laodiceans be on fire and totally committed, trusting God in all things, and working to build his kingdom. Surely the creator of all things, the God of love, ought to be the focus of such passion and desire.

But why would Jesus prefer the Laodiceans be cold? That seems odd. Why would Jesus prefer people not know him at all, or even hate him, to simple indifference? In the gospel of John, we see repeatedly that with Jesus there is no fence straddling—no room for indifference. One believes or one does not believe. One path leads to the light, the other remains in the darkness. One way leads to life, the other to death. And it is Jesus who is "the way, and the truth, and the life" (John 14:6).

In John's gospel and this message to the Laodiceans, the concept of "lukewarm Christian" is an oxymoron. It makes no sense. How could someone have genuinely been born from above (John 3), have given their life over to Jesus Christ, and yet be indifferent about the whole thing? At least Jesus knows where he stands with a person who is either hot or cold.

Many who come to church are like I once was—present but apathetic, not allowing God into any part of my life beyond Sunday morning. A little worship here and there suits some just fine. But Jesus stands at the door, knocking, waiting for us to open it, not just peek through the crack.

God Never Gives Up—Neither Should We

I do not know whether you would call the Jews exiled to Babylonia hot, cold, or lukewarm. Shattered and lost would probably be more accurate. They had been relocated over a thousand miles from Jerusalem with no prospects of returning. They believed that they were being punished for their abandonment of God. In essence, they were headed to prison to serve out a life sentence in bondage.

Yet, this letter from the prophet Jeremiah bears a message from God that even though the generation sent into exile will not return, their children will come back to Jerusalem. This passage is grounded upon a faithful God who never gives up on promises made. And God promises the people a "future with hope" (Jeremiah 29:11).

We might think that God would simply reach out and accomplish all this. God shouldn't need help. "I know the plans I have for you" (v. 11). Yet, these very plans will be shaped and affected by the people. When they call upon God and pray to him . . . then God will hear them (v. 12). The people will find God, and God will find them, but they are to seek God with their heart (v. 13).

There is a deep mystery here that speaks to the profound love that God has for us. You and I, weak and confused though we may be, influence the plans and the actions of God. It is true that our faith is a gift from God so that no one can boast about it (Ephesians 2:8-9), and yet we are to search for God. We are to pray. We are to open the door. As scholar Anthony Saldarini puts it in his commentary on Jeremiah:

> None of that may be quite logical, but it is that peculiar biblical claim about human freedom and divine initiative, or, if you will, divine freedom and human will. . . . God's will and freedom do not run rampant over human words and deeds—good or bad—nor does human intentionality so control what happens that God is unable to affect the divine purposes. What "happens" occurs within that tension. So we count on God to be God and we pray to God in order to bring that about.[1]

Pray and Search

At one point in my life, I was lost. So lost that I did something I think I had never done before. I got on my knees and prayed. I prayed that God would pull me close, would give me direction and purpose. In short, rescue me.

And God did rescue me. Over a period of a few months, God began to move me out of my lukewarm state and brought my wife into my life. By the grace of God, I abandoned my indifference toward God and embraced the life-fulfilling passion that comes from an ever-growing relationship with our Lord.

---

1. Anthony Saldarini, "Jeremiah" in *The New Interpreter's Bible: General Articles & Introduction, Commentary, & Reflections for Each Book of the Bible Including the Apocryphal/Deuterocanonical Books in Twelve Volumes, vol. 6* (Nashville, TN: Abingdon, 2001), p. 796.

People sometimes come to me to talk about that time in my life, for they themselves are lukewarm and lost. My advice to them is always the same: pray and do. Pray and then do the things you would do if you felt the passion you want to feel. Attend worship each week. Join a Sunday School or a Bible study. Find a place to serve on a regular basis. There is infinite variety in how this plays out in our lives, but the basics have always been the same—pray and do.

For a Deeper Understanding

Jeremiah's Letter

As the unrelenting pressure of the Babylonian empire fell on the Jews in Jerusalem nearly 600 years before Jesus, Nebuchadnezzar began sending them into exile. A large wave left for Babylonia in 597 BC, ten years before the final destruction of Jerusalem and the temple. This passage from the book of Jeremiah is part of a letter Jeremiah wrote while still in Jerusalem to those Jews in exile.

The message from God that Jeremiah delivers in the letter is grounded in future hope, though not the immediate moment. The Jews have been exiled to a distant land. They are instructed to go ahead and build homes and raise their families. They are even to pray that Babylon prospers, for then they will prosper as well. It will be decades before God brings them home.

However, the message also carries a warning. The people are not to trust lying "prophets and diviners" amongst them. Their visions and dreams are not to be trusted. We aren't told the specifics, but there were false prophets in Israel and there are false prophets among those exiled in Babylon. Based on the conflicts between Jeremiah and some of the false prophets, it seems most likely that the deceivers were promising a quick end to the exile.

The Seven Churches of Revelation

Revelation is a biblical book that people either seem to be fascinated by or seem to simply avoid in confusion. Some read it as if it is a movie script and wait for it to play out. Others see no message in Revelation relevant to our contemporary lives. However, in truth, Revelation is writing of extraordinary power and profound meaning for us all. It is "God-breathed" just as much as the other 65 books of the Bible. Indeed, some of the most moving and best-known scenes in all of Scripture are found in Revelation. After the opening vision of Christ in the first chapter, John's vision turns to seven letters from Christ to actual churches in western Asia Minor (modern-day Turkey), one of which is the letter to the church at Laodicea.

Each of the seven Christian communities (Ephesus, Smyrna, Pergamum, Thyatira, Sardis, Philadelphia, and Laodicea) gets a different message from Jesus. A good exercise is to read each letter and ask yourself which would be addressed to your church. The specifics of the letters are not always easy to understand, but the thrust of each is clear. The Christians in Smyrna are encouraged in their suffering and poverty. They are rich in what matters. The Philadelphians are encouraged in their patient endurance. Jesus' words to these churches, when laid against the warnings given to the wealthy Laodiceans, remind us that for 2,000 years the way of Christ has been marked by suffering, not prosperity.

Chapter 2

Take It and Eat

Matthew 6:25, 33
Therefore I tell you, do not worry about your life, what you will eat or what you will drink, or about your body, what you will wear. Is not life more than food, and the body more than clothing? . . . But strive first for the kingdom of God and his righteousness, and all these things will be given to you as well.

2 Timothy 3:16–17 (MSG)
Every part of Scripture is God-breathed and useful one way or another— showing us truth, exposing our rebellion, correcting our mistakes, training us to live God's way. Through the Word we are put together and shaped up for the tasks God has for us.

Revelation 10:8–9
Then the voice that I had heard from heaven spoke to me again, saying, "Go, take the scroll that is open in the hand of the angel who is standing on the sea and on the land." So I went to the angel and told him to give me the little scroll; and he said to me, "Take it, and eat; it will be bitter to your stomach, but sweet as honey in your mouth."

Divided Loyalties

We will find the life we have always wanted when we are of a single mind with an overarching purpose, focused on God and his kingdom.

Do you ever feel pulled in several directions at the same time? Your job wants you. Your family wants you. Your friends want you. God wants you. Do you ever feel that your life is made of layers of secrets, as you strive to compartmentalize your behavior, dividing your mind and attention in order to please everyone or meet expectations?

The answer, of course, is that we all feel that way from time to time and, too often, much of the time. The conflicting demands on our priorities can be overwhelming, so much so that we end up with no priorities at all. Our loyalties are divided. Our hearts and minds are divided. We end up stressed out, anxious, ill, and generally miserable. So, what do we do?

One Thing

In his wonderful book, *The Life You've Always Wanted*, pastor John Ortberg talks frankly about his own experience of a divided life and the difficulty of seeking "first for the kingdom of God."[2] Even Jack Palance, in the movie *City Slickers*, understands that the secret to life is "one thing."[3] When Jesus admonishes Martha for getting upset that her sister Mary isn't helping in the kitchen, Jesus reminds her that "there is need of only one thing" (Luke 10:38–42).

Sometimes circumstances help us to focus on "one thing" and grasp its power. A church colleague and I were talking about an upcoming sermon series. She told me that a recent snow day became an extraordinary and holy day for her. She had been playing around with a few ideas for a Lenten sermon series based on the gospel of John. Freed from the usual daily routines, she found that as she worked on the series she lost all track of time. For hours she encountered God with great power. Blessedly, I've had similar experiences as I've written studies or prepared classes. I wish it happened more often.

We can all lose track of time in a variety of experiences. But losing yourself in Scripture is hard to describe. It is holy and it is powerful. For in that time, your heart and mind are focused like a laser on God and the things of God. This complete immersion can happen during Scripture reading, in worship, or in service. Wouldn't it be wonderful if that focus on the "one thing" characterized our entire life, not just all too brief portions of it? Our priorities would be clearer and our loyalties undivided.

Finding Focus

Getting rid of what James calls our "double-mindedness" requires our transformation, the "renewing of our minds" (Romans 12:2). Renewal re-

---

2. Matthew 6:33. One of my favorite authors has long been Philip Yancey. When someone asks me for a book recommendation, I'll often mention Yancey. He is a thoughtful and honest Christian. John Ortberg is fast rivaling Yancey. He too is frank about his own experience with God. I hope that you'll find the time to read his book, *The Life You've Always Wanted: Spiritual Disciplines for Ordinary People* (Grand Rapids, MI: Zondervan, 2009).

3. *City Slickers* (Castle Rock Entertainment, 1991).

quires developing practices that will help to transform us. Ortberg writes, "An indispensable practice is to have our minds re-formed by immersing them in Scripture. . . . So how do we read the Bible in a way that will purify our hearts and help us to live as Jesus would in our place?"[4] Scripture, illumined by the Holy Spirit, helps us to clear away all the debris from our minds and hearts, so that we can focus on Jesus' "one thing."

The striking image from the Revelation passage helps us to grasp that we must take Scripture into us. We are to chew over it and consume it, so that it can nourish our growth. Three times in the Bible an angel hands a scroll to a prophet and tells him to eat it.[5] The prophets are not just to read or hear God's Word, or just understand it, or even just apply it. These people are to eat Scripture, to take it inside themselves so it gets into every part of their person and being.

All this became clearer for pastor Eugene Peterson[6] when he saw his dog working over a bone, slowly chewing and growling. Not long after, he was reading Isaiah 31:4, where a lion "growls" over his prey. It was one of those aha! moments. The Hebrew word translated as "growl" is usually translated "meditate" in the Old Testament. So, there's the question for us: How often do we take the time to "growl" over Scripture? How often do we chew on it, take it inside ourselves, so that we are transformed, not merely informed.

"Take It, and Eat"

How do we "growl" over Scripture? How do we read for transformation, not just information? Ortberg offers some suggestions:

- Ask God to meet you in Scripture
- Read the Bible in a repentant spirit
- Meditate on a fairly brief passage or narrative
- Take one thought or verse with you through the day
- Allow this thought to become part of your memory[7]

Make this a daily practice. There are no shortcuts to the life you've always wanted, but there is great joy in the journey.

---

4. Ortberg, p.178.
5. Jeremiah 15:16, Ezekiel 2:8-3:3, Revelation 10:9-10..
6. Eugene H. Peterson, *Eat This Book: A Conversation in the Art of Spiritual Reading* (Grand Rapids, MI: Eerdmans, 2009).
7. Ortberg, p.182-191.

For a Deeper Understanding

Reading with Heart & Mind

In addition to Ortberg's suggestions, here are a few more strategies for transformational reading:

- Read the story or passage twice during the day, once in the morning and once in the evening. This will help you to keep the narrative in your heart and mind throughout the day, living with it, and letting it work within you.

- Keep some index cards with your Bible. Each day write down the phrase or verse in the passage that is most meaningful to you. Keep this card with you and glance at it once in a while throughout the day. For example, you could set it near your computer or on the kitchen counter so it catches your eye from time to time.

- Find a discussion partner. This needs to be someone with whom you can talk over the scripture several times during the week. This might be your spouse or a friend. Sharing your thoughts and hearing those of someone else is a key way of getting into the story or passage.

Which translation should I read?

There are many excellent English translations of the Bible. My church most often uses the New Revised Standard Version (NRSV). The translation team sought to be as close to the ancient Hebrew and Greek as reasonably possible. In their words, the translators sought to be "as literal as possible, as free as necessary." Consequently, the NRSV can be a little difficult to understand in certain passages.

While I recommend using the NRSV, it is helpful to reach for a more approachable translation at times. The New Living Translation (NLT) is a good choice. You might also enjoy reading from Eugene Peterson's biblical paraphrase, The Message.[8] I find that The Message sometimes has an immediacy and emotional effect that I don't get from the NRSV or even Today's New International Version (TNIV). Bear in mind, however, that to get an "easier" translation, the translators have to get further and further

---

8. Eugene H. Peterson, *The Message: The Bible in Contemporary Language* (Carol Stream, IL: NavPress, 2005).

from the original Hebrew and Greek. Eugene Peterson is a knowledgeable scholar, but paraphrasing ancient languages with modern English presents big challenges.

So, I'd go with the NRSV mainly and supplement your reading with The Message. Specifically, I recommend you read the passage twice each day, once using the NRSV and once using The Message.

Training vs. Trying

Philippians 3:12–16 (MSG)
I'm not saying that I have this all together, that I have it made. But I am well on my way, reaching out for Christ, who has so wondrously reached out for me. Friends, don't get me wrong: By no means do I count myself an expert in all of this, but I've got my eye on the goal, where God is beckoning us onward—to Jesus. I'm off and running, and I'm not turning back. So let's keep focused on that goal, those of us who want everything God has for us. If any of you have something else in mind, something less than total commitment, God will clear your blurred vision—you'll see it yet! Now that we're on the right track, let's stay on it.

1 Corinthians 9:24–27 (MSG)
You've all been to the stadium and seen the athletes race. Everyone runs; one wins. Run to win. All good athletes train hard. They do it for a gold medal that tarnishes and fades. You're after one that's gold eternally. I don't know about you, but I'm running hard for the finish line. I'm giving it everything I've got. No lazy living for me! I'm staying alert and in top condition. I'm not going to get caught napping, telling everyone else all about it and then missing out myself.

When Trying Is Not Enough

What's the difference between making a New Year's resolution and keeping one? It is training versus trying.

Poking fun at the fondness for comparing life to football, baseball, golf, or any other sport has become standard. But even 2,000 years ago, the Apostle Paul couldn't help himself from making the same analogy. It isn't hard to find the metaphor in Paul's letters. We don't know if Paul was an athlete himself or if he was fond of athletics or if he simply understood their importance in the Greco-Roman world that gave us the Olympics. But Paul did know that there is much that we can learn about life, the Christian life, from the games we play. He reminds us to keep our "eye on the goal," stay "on the right track," make "a total commitment," "run the race, "run hard," stay in "top condition," and "train hard."

In his book, *The Life You've Always Wanted*, John Ortberg uses a sports metaphor himself.[9] Suppose you woke up tomorrow morning and decided to run a marathon. You put on some running shoes, don the right apparel, and head out the door to begin your 26.2-mile run. Could you do it? What if you tried hard? Really, really hard? If you gave it the proverbial "110%"? The obvious answer is no, of course not. No matter how hard I may try, I would not simply head out the door and run 26 miles. If I want to run a marathon, I'm going to have to train for it. Effort and intention will not cut it.

When I was in the Air Force, I taught people to fly jet airplanes. There again, effort was essential. It took a year of intense training to create a US Air Force pilot. Nobody flies a jet by effort alone, or on their first try, or second, or tenth. They train. They prepare.

So it is with all the great endeavors of our lives. It takes learning and training and discipline. And what could be a greater endeavor than becoming the person God has created each of us to be? A loving disciple of Jesus with the power, as Dallas Willard puts it, "to work the works of the kingdom."[10] When Paul wrote to the Christians of Corinth, Greece, he was training hard in the things of God. He knew that without training, our resolve to be trusting and obedient disciples dissolves into failed resolutions.

Training for the Fruit

Of course, it is one thing to say that we are going to train ourselves to be a mature disciple of Jesus, but it's another to know how. In his letter to the Galatians, Paul tells the Christians that those who are led by the Spirit will bear the fruit of the Spirit: "love, joy, peace, patience, kindness, generosity, faithfulness, gentleness, and self-control" (Galatians 5:22-23). But how do you train yourself to be gentle or to be joyful? I can try to be patient (boy, have I tried . . . and failed), but how do I train myself to be patient?

Ortberg reminds us that we need to slow down if we are going to embrace the life God offers us. But he also acknowledges that he too suffers from our culture's "hurry-up" sickness. I know just what he means. I

9.   Ortberg, p.41.
10.   Dallas Willard, *The Divine Conspiracy: Rediscovering Our Hidden Life in God* (New York NY, HarperCollins, 1998), p.368.

make a careful and complex calculation as I arrive with my basket at the grocery store checkout. I scan the lines, estimate the speed of the checkers, and choose my line. Too often, I end up enormously frustrated because my "competition" in the nearby line gets out quicker than I do. My wife and I have been known to stand in two ticket lines at the movies. Whoever gets to the window first buys the tickets! Yes, it is a sickness. After all, what do I really do with those five minutes I might save? Surely less than I imagine.

How do I possibly learn patience? How do I learn to slow down and catch my breath? Ortberg has tried picking the longest line on purpose, hoping he would learn to like it. I have not yet worked up the strength of will to emulate his training method. But I do know that if I do not actually train myself to be more patient, I will never get there. Yes, God helps me in this, but I must still train to be patient.

How about prayer? Christians with deep and meaningful prayer lives do not arrive there by accident. They learn to pray. They train to pray. They are disciplined, praying even when they do not feel like it or think they have nothing to say. The same for Bible reading and study. Have you ever taken a Bible study with other Christians or are you still just trying on your own to discover the life-changing power of Scripture?

Doing versus Being

In *The Divine Conspiracy*, Dallas Willard helps us to see that this training is not so much about doing as it is about being.[11] Our goal is to be evermore Christlike. In our training and our trying, our aim is not just to control our behavior, but to be transformed. My goal is to be a patient person, not just to behave patiently. We want to be joyful. We want to be loving. We want to be kind. We seek transformation, not merely better performance. We can never live Sermon-on-the-Mount lives by reducing Jesus' teachings to a list of rules. If the life we seek is a transformed life, we need a metamorphosis.

The chart that follows illustrates the way we progress from one dimension in our life with God to another and then to another. As we move from one level to the next we are growing in Christlikeness; we are becoming the persons God created us to be. Spiritual disciplines are practices that change the inner self, that help us toward the inner transformation of heart and soul. Thus, these disciplines are the training tools that Christians have found to be necessary: celebration, prayer, Bible study, servanthood, and

---

11. Willard.

confession. There are many different lists of disciplines, but they all share a commitment to training for God's kingdom, not merely striving. These disciplines are the practices that create the life we seek.

For a Deeper Understanding[12]

FIVE DIMENSIONS OF OUR LIFE IN CHRIST

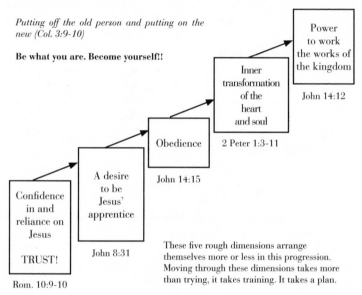

Putting off the old person and putting on the new (Col. 3:9-10)

Be what you are. Become yourself!!

Power to work the works of the kingdom

John 14:12

Inner transformation of the heart and soul

2 Peter 1:3-11

Obedience

John 14:15

A desire to be Jesus' apprentice

John 8:31

Confidence in and reliance on Jesus

TRUST!

Rom. 10:9-10

These five rough dimensions arrange themselves more or less in this progression. Moving through these dimensions takes more than trying, it takes training. It takes a plan.

from Dallas Willard's book, *A Divine Conspiracy*

---

12.   Willard, p.367.

Chapter 4

Pass the Salt

Matthew 5:1–2, 13–16
When Jesus saw the crowds, he went up the mountain; and after he sat down, his disciples came to him. Then he began to speak, and taught them, saying:

[What follows are known as the Beatitudes, e.g., "Blessed are the peace-makers, for they will be called children of God . . . ."]

You are the salt of the earth; but if salt has lost its taste, how can its saltiness be restored? It is no longer good for anything, but is thrown out and trampled under foot.

You are the light of the world. A city built on a hill cannot be hid. No one after lighting a lamp puts it under the bushel basket, but on the lampstand, and it gives light to all in the house. In the same way, let your light shine before others, so that they may see your good works and give glory to your Father in heaven.

Each of us has chosen to be a disciple of Jesus Christ. But what sort of disciple will we be?

Why Salt?

Jesus challenges his disciples to be the salt that seasons and the light that illuminates. Salt has many uses. Some positive, some negative. A swim in the ocean is always good for healing small nicks and scrapes. All animals need a certain amount of salt in their diet to live. Who doesn't crave salty snacks? Of course, too much salt also kills. The Dead Sea is sometimes referred to as the Salt Sea. Photographs of its shore reveal rocks and gravel covered with layers of dried, white salts. Nothing can live there. The salts have squeezed all life out of the environment.

Drawing on the contrasting properties, the biblical writers generously use images of salt. Sometimes salt is used as an image of seasoning, preserving, or purifying. But salt is also used as an image of death, desolation, or even a curse. God's covenant with his people is occasionally referred to as a covenant of salt, drawing upon the preserving qualities of salt (Leviticus 2:13; Numbers 18:19; 2 Chronicles 13:5). Newborn babies were rubbed with salt as a symbol of new beginnings. Paul urged the Christians to speak with "grace, seasoned with salt" (Colossians 4:6 NIV). Yet, more than a millennia before Paul, Abilmelech spread salt across the ground of a razed city as a sign of a curse (Judges 9:45).[13]

In Matthew's Gospel, Jesus begins the Sermon on the Mount with the Beatitudes, a very moving reversal of the world's value systems. Then he immediately speaks to the disciples about their own vocation, their own call to actually be God's people, a community grounded firmly in the kingdom of God. Jesus uses three metaphors to make his point. The first is salt, the second is light, and the third is the city.[14]

Contrasts and Choices

Jesus calls upon the contrasting uses of salt. On the one hand, salt gives life, but on the other, it can render something useless. Which sort of disciple will John, Andrew, Peter, and the other be? Will they be good for something, or, like the tasteless salt, will they be good for nothing? The choice is stark and clear. It is one way or the other. No ambiguity.

To make the same point again, Jesus uses the image of light. Will his disciples hide their light or will they raise it up and let it shine so that the whole world can see? Which will it be? And why are they to be a shining light? So that all people in all places can see, through the good works of the disciples, that God is God and that Jesus is Lord of all creation.

Likewise, a city that sits on a hill is going to be seen by everyone, whether the city wants to be seen or not. The world will be looking at the disciples whether they want to be seen or not. Our life is a witness to God whether we want it to be or not.

New Testament scholar M. Eugene Boring writes:

---

13. A fascinating reference book is the *Dictionary of Biblical Imagery*, published by Inter-Varsity Press. It is a large encyclopedic look at the Bible's many images, metaphors, symbols, figures of speech, and so forth. Leland Ryken, James C. Wilhoit, and Tremper Longman III, eds. (Downers Grove, IL: InterVarsity, 1998).

14. Jesus often uses multiple images or stories to make the same point. This is a Hebrew way of teaching. You see this even in Hebrew poetry, such as the Psalms. We tend to think of poetry as involving rhyming with sounds. The psalmists would often rhyme using parallel ways of expressing a single point. For example, Psalm 19:1 (NIV) opens, "The heavens declare the glory of God; the skies proclaim the work of his hands." The two lines together, like synonyms, express a single thought—all of creation points to the truth that is a creator. In the same way, Jesus uses salt, light, and city as metaphors that speak to discipleship.

The salt and light sayings picture mission as inherent to discipleship, as saltiness is essential to salt and shining is essential to light. For salt, being salty is not optional. With these three metaphors of salt, light, and city, the Matthean Jesus strikes a death blow to all religion that is purely personal and private. . . . The community that lives by the power of unostentatious prayer in the inner room (Matthew 6:6) is not an introverted secret society shielding itself from the world, but is a city set on a hill whose authentic life cannot be concealed.[15]

In these three brief metaphors - salt, light, city on a hill - Jesus appeals to our imaginations, helping us to grasp the radical, outwardly focused nature of the Christian life. Our lives, our good works, are to be like pictures of God's love that can be seen by all those who have not yet placed their trust in the Lord Jesus Christ.

For a Deeper Understanding

The Sermon on the Mount

How often we return to the Sermon on the Mount from Matthew's Gospel, as we should. This is the largest single block of Jesus' teaching in the New Testament, spanning chapters 5–7 in Matthew.

The teachings directly spell out what it means to live a life under the rule of God. Jesus had more to say about the kingdom of God than any other subject. In these three chapters, we have the fullest statement of what life in the kingdom is really like. And it is profoundly counter-cultural.

The Sermon on the Mount turns the world's values on its head. Up becomes down. In becomes out. Power becomes weakness. Jesus is not laying out some idealized picture of what life might be like someday when he returns. Rather, Jesus is setting out his expectations of his disciples. They are a community formed by God and empowered by God's Spirit. The Sermon on the Mount is a sort of guidebook to life in Christian community.

Take a look at how Jesus closes the Sermon on the Mount (Matthew 7:24–27). He tells the story of two people who build homes. One builds the house on rock so that it could withstand storms. The other built on a foundation of sand that was easily washed away. The one who builds on rock is the one who hears Jesus' words and does them. The one who builds on sand is the one who hears Jesus' words but does not do them. The choice is clear and ours to make. The consequences are also clear.

---

15.   Eugene M. Boring, "Matthew" in *NIB*, vol. 7 (Nashville, TN: Abingdon, 1995), p.137.

"Give Glory to Your Father"

Glory is one of those words that we use in church all the time. It is found throughout the Bible. We know that giving glory to God is a good thing, but what does "giving glory" really mean?

To get at this, we need to begin by understanding a little more about Jesus' world. Mediterranean societies, including Roman and Jewish culture, were built around a strong sense of community and family. People's lives were driven by the ambition to accumulate honor and to avoid shame—both social concepts. Money was helpful only to the extent that it might enable you to acquire prestige and reputation by, for example, extending favors to others.

Honor is the value of a person in his or her own eyes plus the person's value in the eyes of others. So honor, the most important commodity in these societies, is the claim to worth along with the social acknowledgement of one's worth. It is who you are plus who other people say you are.

Giving glory to a person (glorifying them) is to lift them up so that everyone can see that they are who they say they are. It is ascribing worth and honor to another. The disciples' good works will enable everyone to see that God is who God says he is—a good and loving God. The lives of the disciples are to be a witness to others. "Glory" is a social term, like honor, shame, prestige, and reputation. Here is another example: Jesus' death on the cross is as shameful a death as any Jew or Roman could imagine (see Philippians 2:5–11). Yet, by raising Jesus from the dead for everyone to see, God glorified Jesus. God ascribed to him worth and honor.

If you would like to learn more about the social world of Jesus' day in order to gain a richer understanding of the New Testament, I suggest you begin with Bruce Malina's *The New Testament World*, now in its third edition.[16] It is pretty eye-opening. For example, one chapter is titled "Envy: The Most Grievous of all Evils." I doubt many of us think of envy that way, even when we read in Mark's Gospel that the chief priests turned Jesus over to Pilate out of envy.

---

16.   Bruce J. Malina, *The New Testament World: Insights from Cultural Anthropology*, 3rd ed. (Louisville, KY: Westminster John Knox Press, 2001).

Decisions, Decisions

Numbers 14:1–10a

Then all the congregation raised a loud cry, and the people wept that night. And all the Israelites complained against Moses and Aaron; the whole congregation said to them, "Would that we had died in the land of Egypt! Or would that we had died in this wilderness! Why is the LORD bringing us into this land to fall by the sword? Our wives and our little ones will become booty; would it not be better for us to go back to Egypt?" So they said to one another, "Let us choose a captain, and go back to Egypt." Then Moses and Aaron fell on their faces before all the assembly of the congregation of the Israelites. And Joshua son of Nun and Caleb son of Jephunneh, who were among those who had spied out the land, tore their clothes and said to all the congregation of the Israelites, "The land that we went through as spies is an exceedingly good land. If the LORD is pleased with us, he will bring us into this land and give it to us, a land that flows with milk and honey. Only, do not rebel against the LORD; and do not fear the people of the land, for they are no more than bread for us; their protection is removed from them, and the LORD is with us; do not fear them." But the whole congregation threatened to stone them.

We are defined by the choices we make. Some are big decisions; most are small. Today, we consider the story of the Israelites and their decision whether to trust God fully or to trust their own wisdom and abilities. Sadly, they made a bad decision.

Ready for Responsibility

After leading the people out of slavery, God met the Hebrews at Mt. Sinai. God revealed himself to them there. He taught them what it meant to be the people of God, that they were to love God and love their neighbor. God told them how to build a dwelling where God would be present with his people in a way that he was present with no other people. They were to be God's "treasured possession."

But, of course, being shaped into God's people meant they were being shaped for responsibility. They were to be the ones through whom God would restore all of humanity to a right relationship with God. God led them from Mt. Sinai to the borders of Canaan so that the Israelites might move into the land that God had promised to Abraham centuries before. Yet despite all that had happened, the people seemed plagued by fears, doubts, and anxieties. Sometimes they went so far as to wish they were still back in Egypt. Far from being responsible people, ready to trust God in all things, time and again they forgot about their escape from Pharaoh and even the food God had rained down upon them from heaven as manna (Exodus 16). They could see only the unknowns ahead and embrace only their fears.

When the Israelites arrived at the borders of Canaan, at God's instruction they sent in a team of spies to check things out. Sensible enough. However, when the spies returned after forty days, they reported that though the land flowed with "milk and honey," the Canaanites were simply too strong and as big as giants. In their fear, the people turned back, some even desiring to return to Egypt. Despite their experiences with God and their experience of God, their faith was weak. They trusted God too little. They weren't really sure that God would or could keep his promises. Indeed, their faith was not really placed in Yahweh, the God of Moses. Rather, their faith was in a god of their own making, a god much too small to trust with life and death. God then tells Moses that because the people have refused to enter the land, they never will. They will have to wander around the Sinai wilderness until the distrustful generation dies off—hence the forty years. God will have Joshua and Caleb, the trusting two, lead the next generation into Canaan. So, the people wander, and wander, and wander. Even Moses himself will not enter the promised land. The people of God will reap the consequences of their fears and distrust.

Three Decisions

In his year-long Bible study *The Grand Sweep*, scholar Ellsworth Kalas draws our attention to three decisions that the Israelites make after leaving Mt. Sinai for the Promised Land.

First, the Israelites make the decision to complain.[17] Abraham Lincoln once observed that people are about as happy as they make up their minds to be. I think he was right. We can wake up each morning and decide

---

17. "How the Drama Develops - (Numbers 7-21)" in *The Grand Sweep: 365 Days from Genesis through Revelation: A Bible Study for Individuals and Groups* (Nashville, TN: Abingdon, 1996).

whether we are going to have a positive outlook that day or a negative one. Yes, the Israelites were anxious and scared as they traveled through the Sinai wilderness, but they could have decided to swallow their grumbling and confidently embrace God's promises.

Second, the Israelites decided to criticize, directing their insecurities and anxieties at Moses. In Numbers 12, Aaron, Moses' brother, and Miriam, Moses' sister, oppose Moses. "What makes him so special?" they think to themselves. But it was God who made Moses special and God's anger burned hot against Aaron and Miriam for their arrogance. Like complaining, criticizing hardly seems like a decision. Yet, we are defined by many such decisions we make every day. Will we hold our tongue or will we lash out? Will we criticize or will we support?

Third, the Israelites decided to retreat. This one is easier to understand as a decision. Would they trust God and enter Canaan despite the fears of their spies or would they rely on their own judgment and turn back? But the grumbling begot the criticizing and the criticizing begot the retreat. Our own lives are like this. Lots of wrong "little" decisions lead inexorably to a wrong "big" decision. Do we really think that we can deny God in the small stuff of our lives and yet trust God in the big stuff? Wise Christians know that the mature Christian life is a life led fully in God's presence, in the small decisions as well as the big ones.

For a Deeper Understanding

God's "Steadfast Love"

Before the Israelites depart Mt. Sinai, God reveals more of himself in a long list of adjectives (Exodus 34:6–7). One of the most striking is God's promise of "steadfast love for the thousandth generation." It is God's steadfast love that the people can and ought to trust when they reach the Promised Land but do not. What does "steadfast love" really mean?

These two words translate the single Hebrew word *hesed*, which is one of the most important words in the Old Testament. It is virtually a one-word summary of Israel's understanding of God. No English word can do it justice, not even two. It is one of those Hebrew words better translated with a paragraph.

Used more than 240 times in the Old Testament, especially in the Psalms, *hesed* conveys love, strength, trust, kindness, mercy, faithfulness, steadfastness, loyalty, truthfulness—all embodied in a covenant relationship. Our word "devotion" perhaps best captures the nuances of *hesed*. God is devoted to his people. The older English translations most often rendered *hesed* as "lovingkindness," an archaic word but a good one.

Hesed is a covenantal word and may also be used to talk about marital love. A marriage is a legal contract but much more. A marriage is a covenant between two people who are expected to demonstrate devotion, trust, and lovingkindness in their relationship. Their devotion to each other is not just a sentiment; it is to be expressed in concrete actions of loving, protecting, and being truthful. Under their covenant, each spouse is obligated to the other and finds great joy in those obligations. They are to abound in steadfast love for each other.

In much the same way, God's *hesed* for his people is expressed in God's acts of mercy and salvation. In Psalm 25, the psalmist proclaims that God's steadfast love has been "from of old." As the psalm unfolds, it is clear that the psalmist has in mind the Exodus, God's deliverance of his people from Egypt. God's love for his people, for us, is seen in his actions. We proclaim a God who acts. The psalmist prays that he would know God's ways so he can, through his actions, be faithful to the covenant just as God has been faithful. After all, this is what covenant partners do. And this is what the Israelites fail to do when they reach the border of Canaan.

Learning for Discipleship

It has been said that biblical illiteracy is a problem in my denomination, The United Methodist Church. This problem is critical, because "United Methodists share with other Christians the conviction that Scripture is the primary source and criterion for Christian doctrine."[18] It is also ironic, as Methodism's founder John Wesley was Oxford-educated and considered himself to be a "man of one book," the Bible. We are called to be a people of that book. In the pages of the Bible, we learn of God's hopes for us and expectations of us. In its pages, we confront the living Lord and learn of his love for us. In its pages, we learn how to live the sort of life that God intended for us. Indeed, Will Willimon reminds us that "a congregation is Christian to the degree that it is confronted by and attempts to form its life in response to the Word of God."[19]

---

18. *The Book of Discipline of the United Methodist Church* (Nashville, TN: The United Methodist Publishing House, 2000), p.78.
19. William H. Willimon, *Shaped by the Bible* (Nashville, TN: Abingdon, 1991), p.11.

A Passionate Life

Luke 24:30–35
When he was at the table with them, he took bread, blessed and broke it, and gave it to them. Then their eyes were opened, and they recognized him; and he vanished from their sight. They said to each other, "Were not our hearts burning within us while he was talking to us on the road, while he was opening the scriptures to us?" That same hour they got up and returned to Jerusalem; and they found the eleven and their companions gathered together. They were saying, "The Lord has risen indeed, and he has appeared to Simon!" Then they told what had happened on the road, and how he had been made known to them in the breaking of the bread.

Acts 18:24–28
Now there came to Ephesus a Jew named Apollos, a native of Alexandria. He was an eloquent man, well-versed in the scriptures. He had been instructed in the Way of the Lord; and he spoke with burning enthusiasm and taught accurately the things concerning Jesus, though he knew only the baptism of John. He began to speak boldly in the synagogue; but when Priscilla and Aquila heard him, they took him aside and explained the Way of God to him more accurately. And when he wished to cross over to Achaia [the Greek peninsula], the believers encouraged him and wrote to the disciples to welcome him. On his arrival he greatly helped those who through grace had become believers, for he powerfully refuted the Jews in public, showing by the scriptures that the Messiah is Jesus.

Passionate Church

In Leo Buscaglia's *Bus 9 to Paradise*, readers are taken on a mythical bus ride toward paradise on earth, looking for ways to embrace the simple joys of life. What struck me most was Buscaglia's observation that joyful people have passions in their lives—activities or interests that make them excited to get up in the morning.[20] On Bus 9 it mattered less what the particular passion was, as simply being passionate about something can lead to a passion-filled life. Buscaglia was right so far as he went, but I've come to learn that the object of our passion matters too. To the point, all of us are created in the image of God so that we might become passionately devoted to God and to one another so that we might become passionate disciples of Jesus Christ.

We must journey toward such passion, toward a much better understanding of what it means to be a disciple of Jesus, and, most importantly, toward a life centered upon our relationships with God and one another. After all, who doesn't want a life filled with enthusiasm, passion, and joy? In this chapter's Scripture passages, we meet several people who must have been surprised by the passion they found welling up in their own hearts.

"Were Not Our Hearts Burning Within Us . . . ?"

On a Sunday afternoon, two disciples were on the road to Emmaus, a town some distance from Jerusalem. They were followers of Jesus from Nazareth and had been in Jerusalem for the tumultuous last week of Jesus' life. They talked busily about all that had happened in the past few days. They were puzzled and confused about how it all had ended on Friday. But then again, some women had made the most amazing claim that morning, that Jesus was alive!

They were joined by a third man as they walked along. The man walked with them and talked with them, explaining why the Messiah had to suffer. When they sat down to the evening meal, the man took the bread, blessed, and broke it, and gave it to them. When they ate, their eyes were open and they knew that the man was Jesus. Later, after Jesus had left them, they realized that their hearts had been burning inside them as they talked with this unknown man.

When we talk about the people of history, whether it is Julius Caesar or George Washington, we are talking about a dead person. But when we talk about Jesus, we are talking about someone who lives, who is still involved in the world and in our lives. We may not be able to sit down with Jesus at the dinner table like the two disciples on the road to Emmaus, but we can have a relationship with Jesus that "burns in our own hearts" as well.

---

20.   Leo F. Buscaglia, *Bus 9 to Paradise* (New York, NY: Ballantine, 1987).

For a Deeper Understanding

"He Spoke with Burning Enthusiasm . . ."

Apollos is one of the lesser known figures in the New Testament. He is a Jewish Christian, both educated and eloquent, from Alexandria, Egypt, the second largest city in the Roman Empire. We first meet Apollos in Ephesus, a very large city on the western coast of modern-day Turkey. He has come there to preach the Gospel of Jesus Christ. He does so knowledgeably and with a "burning enthusiasm." It seems though that Apollos has some things to learn (who doesn't!). He has not been taught well about the Christian practice of baptism, for he knows only about the baptism practiced by John the Baptist. However, being a devoted and passionate disciple, Apollos is eager to learn. In Ephesus, a husband-wife team, Aquila and Priscilla, take Apollos aside and teach him more about the Christian faith. Better equipped for his ministry, Apollos then leaves Ephesus and heads for Corinth, where he will continue to play a prominent role in the young church. So far as we know, Apollos' passion never subsides. More than fifteen years after Apollos first appeared in Ephesus, Paul urges Titus to see that Apollos lacks nothing in his work of proclaiming the Gospel (Titus 3:13).

Finding the Passion

Reading stories from the New Testament of disciples with burning hearts is one thing but, for many of us, "burning hearts" would rarely describe our lives as Christians. Perhaps we feel the burn once in a while, but too many Christians don't find much to be truly passionate about in their life, much less in their faith.

The path of genuine, passionate, discipleship may not always be easy, but it has been well trod. And from our passionate lives as disciples of Jesus Christ will emerge a passionate church ever more equipped and ready to be the light to the world, to throw head, heart, and hands into the joyful work of helping others to live within God's kingdom and to enjoy a passion they never imagined. Such is the power of burning hearts.

Chapter 7

Messengers of the Churches

Romans 10:14–15

But how are they to call on one in whom they have not believed? And how are they to believe in one of whom they have never heard? And how are they to hear without someone to proclaim him? And how are they to proclaim him unless they are sent? As it is written, "How beautiful are the feet of those who bring good news!"

2 Corinthians 8:16–23

But thanks be to God who put in the heart of Titus the same eagerness for you that I myself have. For he not only accepted our appeal, but since he is more eager than ever, he is going to you of his own accord. With him we are sending the brother who is famous among all the churches for his proclaiming the good news; and not only that, but he has also been appointed by the churches to travel with us while we are administering this generous undertaking for the glory of the Lord himself and to show our goodwill. We intend that no one should blame us about this generous gift that we are administering, for we intend to do what is right not only in the Lord's sight but also in the sight of others. And with them we are sending our brother whom we have often tested and found eager in many matters, but who is now more eager than ever because of his great confidence in you. As for Titus, he is my partner and co-worker in your service; as for our brothers, they are messengers of the churches, the glory of Christ

The Good News

I have mentioned before that I am drawn to Paul's letters. I think, in large part, this is because Paul is doing the hard work of building up Christian communities. He is encouraging, instructing, and even rebuking these young communities as he goes about the work of the kingdom—inviting people in, welcoming them, challenging them to be true disciples of Christ and summoning them to their own work for the kingdom. These passages

26

give us a glimpse inside Paul's exhortations to proclaim the Good News of Jesus Christ and to be eager messengers of the church in all that they do.

It is worth reviewing what we mean by the Good News, or more precisely, what Paul means. The Good News (*evangelion* in the Greek, also translated "gospel") is not a summary of Jesus' teachings nor a synopsis of his life and not even the comfort of knowing that Jesus loves us. Granted, all of that is good and much of it is news to many of us, but it is not what Paul nor the other New Testament writers mean by "Good News." The Good News is the proclamation to the entire world that Jesus is Lord. It is no more complicated than that and no less profound. It is a public proclamation of something we claim is true. This world, indeed all of creation, has one Master and that person is Jesus. It is to him and him alone that every knee should bow (Philippians 2:6–11). This is the Good News that transcends all other news because unless it is so, the world and all its inhabitants are adrift in a cosmos that is still lost. Priest and scholar Richard Burridge writes, "Paul says remarkably little about Jesus' ministry, and rarely quotes his teaching. Instead, he sees the whole nexus of Jesus' life, death, and resurrection as a totality. In the 'Christ Event' God has acted to save men and women—and the whole cosmos. It is the central pivot of the ages."[21]

But how is this Good News to be believed, to be trusted? In a series of four rhetorical questions, the ever-practical Paul urges the Christians in Rome to understand that for the Good News to be trusted and embraced by people, it must first be proclaimed to them, and it can only be proclaimed if there are those willing to go out and do the proclaiming. But who is to do this proclaiming?

The Messengers

The words can get a bit tricky here. In 2 Corinthians 8:23, Paul describes Titus and the unnamed brothers as *apostolos*, which the NRSV kindly translates here as "messengers." We often mistakenly assume that when the New Testament writers refer to apostles they mean only the twelve[22] plus Paul. But, in truth, the New Testament uses a wide range of meanings for "apostle," which is simply the Greek word for "messenger," or more fully, "one who is sent with full authority." For example, Paul refers to himself as an apostle of Jesus Christ, specially commissioned by the risen Lord just as

---

21. Richard A. Burridge, "And in Jesus Christ, His Only Son, Lord" in *Exploring and Proclaiming the Apostles' Creed*, ed. Roger E. Van Harn (Grand Rapids, MI: Eerdmans, 2004), p.60.

22. You may recall that Matthias was chosen to replace Judas (Acts 1:26).

were the original twelve. And he clearly sees this as differentiating himself from other Christians. But he also lists Junia, almost certainly a woman, as "prominent among the apostles" (Romans 16:7) and lists "apostles" as among the gifts given to the church (Ephesians 4:11).

Christians have disagreed about exactly what to make of the varying distinctions among *apostolos* in the New Testament. Roman Catholics and Pentecostals have arrived at very different conclusions and Methodists are somewhere in the middle. Yet, all Christians find unity in Christ's call for us to be the light to the world, to go and make disciples, to be messengers of the Good News. We may be given different gifts of proclamation, some of us may be better at deeds than at words, but we are all sent.

The Glory of Christ

Paul writes that these messengers of the churches are the "glory of Christ." Glory is the image of God, the divine transcendence, made visible to others, to the world. It is about seeing God. Thus, Jesus is the glory of God, for he makes God visible—see Jesus, see God. The cross is the glory of God, for it makes God's redeeming love visible. Titus and the unnamed brothers are Christ's glory because others can see God at work in them and through them. Their dedication and devotion to their God-given vocation glorifies Jesus Christ because it helps the world to see that Jesus is who they claim he is, namely, Lord and Savior of all.

We too are messengers of the church, called to invite others to the Lord's table. We too are the glory of Christ, for our friends and neighbors can see God at work in us as we lovingly and enthusiastically invite them to join us!

For a Deeper Understanding

Second Corinthians has been of enormous importance to the church. For example, chapter 3 gives us the fullest presentation of the Christian categories of old and new covenants (also known as "testaments"). Yet, in some ways the letter seems a bit of a hodge-podge, ranging across diverse topics and styles. Many scholars believe that 2 Corinthians is actually portions of several letters to the church in Corinth that were merged into a single document.

Despite questions about its unity, Orthodox scholar Edith Humphrey writes that the theological drive in the letter is integration. "Above all others, this letter reminds us that pastoral, academic, and theological roles are best held together. Paul addresses the particular questions of his beloved church without losing sight of the larger picture."[23]

Paul seeks to resolve problems with church authority and structure. He calls the people to holy lives in which even the mundane is God's. He urges them toward generosity as he reminds them of Jesus' own "generous act" (8:9). Paul defends his own ministry against those he believes are trying to pull the people away from the one true God. Through it all, Paul seeks to build up this still-fragile community of believers.

---

23. Edith M. Humphrey, "2 Corinthians, Book of" in *Dictionary of Theological Interpretation of the Bible*, general ed. Kevin J. Vanhoozer (Grand Rapids, MI: Baker Academic, 2005). p.141.

Chapter 8

The Miracle of Sharing

Matthew 14:13–21
Now when Jesus heard this, he withdrew from there in a boat to a deserted place by himself. But when the crowds heard it, they followed him on foot from the towns. When he went ashore, he saw a great crowd; and he had compassion for them and cured their sick. When it was evening, the disciples came to him and said, "This is a deserted place, and the hour is now late; send the crowds away so that they may go into the villages and buy food for themselves." Jesus said to them, "They need not go away; you give them something to eat." They replied, "We have nothing here but five loaves and two fish." And he said, "Bring them here to me." Then he ordered the crowds to sit down on the grass. Taking the five loaves and the two fish, he looked up to heaven, and blessed and broke the loaves, and gave them to the disciples, and the disciples gave them to the crowds. And all ate and were filled; and they took up what was left over of the broken pieces, twelve baskets full. And those who ate were about five thousand men, besides women and children.

A Simple Story

It is not hard to understand why children like the Bible story about the loaves and fishes. It is easy to visualize and we all can relate to the crowd. A huge and hungry crowd is gathered on a Galilean hillside. Having only five loaves of bread and two fish, Jesus blesses and miraculously multiplies the food so it is sufficient to feed perhaps 20,000 people with food left over! (Though the story is often referred to as the "feeding of the five thousand," the figure refers only to the men in the crowd, so 20,000 is a reasonable estimate.)

But children are not the only ones to have treasured this story. Of all the miracles recounted in the gospels, this is the only miracle that appears in all four gospels! In fact, there are two more accounts of Jesus miraculously feeding thousands. As you might expect, each gospel writer tells the story a little differently. John tells us that a boy brought forward the few loaves and fishes. More than the others, John's telling of the meal evokes memories of the Exodus and manna and of Jesus' last supper with his disciples. Mark has more detail and emphasizes Jesus' compassion. More explicitly than the others, Luke ties together the disciples' mission to build the kingdom and the power of Jesus' work with the crowds. This is how it is with the gospel accounts. Matthew, Mark, Luke, and John may all work with the same material, but each use it to paint a distinctive portrait of Jesus.

Matthew's Story

So, what is the attraction of this particular miracle? Why, of all the miracles Jesus performed during his public ministry, is this the only one preserved by all four gospel writers? Yes, it is spectacular, but no more so than Jesus' resuscitation of Lazarus after he had been dead four days. There were other large crowds that witnessed Jesus' miracles, though probably few as large as 20,000. Perhaps Matthew's simple account will help us understand the significance to the gospel writers of this particular story.

After the execution of his cousin John, Jesus goes off to be alone, even resorting to the use of a boat to find solitude. But, of course, the crowds track him down and gather around him as soon as he sets foot on shore. Jesus is not upset with the crowds who press in on him; rather, he has compassion for them and cures their sick. Late in the day, the disciples come to Jesus, pointing out that they are out in the middle of nowhere and it is time for everyone to head off and find something to eat in the nearby villages. But Jesus says no; everyone can stay. Though only five loaves of bread and two fish can be found, Jesus looks to heaven, blesses the food, hands it to his disciples. Jesus is not referred to again in this story. Perhaps the significance of this miracle story lies here.

It is Jesus who takes the bread, blesses it, breaks it, and multiplies it, but it is the disciples who actually distribute the food, feed the crowds, and collect the leftovers. Jesus is the power behind the feeding, but the disciples are the ones who do the work. Jesus doesn't wave a magic wand over the crowd so that food might appear in everyone's lap or so that the hungry tummies will be magically full. This is why the miraculous feeding is in all four gospels. The entire miracle story is a metaphor for how Jesus will work. Jesus' work will be done by others, during his ministry and after his death. Jesus is teaching his disciples what his ministry is all about. He doesn't just tell them, he shows them. The work of building God's kingdom will be done through the disciples, then and now.

Sharing the Miracle

From God's choosing of Abraham, to the feeding of the thousands, to the work that Christians all over the world are doing in the present day, it has always been this way. God is not a god-of-the-magic-wand. God's purposes are worked out through us, not despite us. Jesus reminds his disciples that they are to be the light of the world. He sends them out to proclaim the kingdom of God and to heal the sick (Luke 9:2). He shows his disciples how this works by handing them the loaves and having them distribute the food. If the crowds are going to get fed, the disciples are going to have to do it. They can't sit around hoping and praying that Jesus will do it for them. The disciples know whose power is at work, but they are also learning that their own hands better get busy.

Why is it this way? Why doesn't God simply wave a wand? Because God is love and we have been created so that we might love God and one another. This love is not mere sentiment or feeling, this love is carried in our compassion, our caring, our service, and our sacrifice.

For a Deeper Understanding

Two Banquets

A key to reading the Bible well is to always look for the context. Put the verse in the paragraph, the paragraph in the immediate story, and then put the story in the context of the stories around it. For example, Matthew puts two banquet stories side-by-side: Herod's banquet (Matthew 14:1–12) and the feeding of the thousands (14:13–21). Herod's banquet ends in death; Jesus' banquet ends in abundance.

John the Baptist was Jesus' cousin. Herod had arrested John and thrown him in prison to shut him up, for John had condemned Herod's incestuous relationship with Herodias, his niece and his brother's wife. (What a family tree that must have been!)

Herod wants John dead but fears the consequences of an execution. He knows that John the Baptist enjoys popular support. However, on Herod's birthday, there is a huge banquet. Herodias' daughter dances for the king and Herod is so taken with her (yes, we are supposed to grasp the decadence in all this!) that he grants her a wish, any wish. The girl asks for the head of John the Baptist on a platter—and Herod delivers. After Jesus' disciples claim John's body and bury it, Jesus withdraws to a boat to be alone.

By putting these stories side-by-side, Matthew draws a stark contrast between the rotten empire of Caesar and the life-giving empire of Christ.

Caesar and all his minions, like Herod, may believe and proclaim that Caesar is Lord, but it is a lie. There is only one Lord, Jesus Christ, and only one kingdom, God's. Caesar may have the power to kill John the Baptist, but it is a power that destroys, not creates. Jesus, the true Lord and Savior, has the power to create where there was nothing. In Caesar, lies death. In Christ, lies life.

PART II
TO TRUST HIM

The Christian faith is about just that—faith. And the very best synonym for faith is the simple word "trust." Because of a few problems with the English language, we easily lose sight of that simple word "trust." We are told we need to believe in Jesus, as in the famous verse, "For God so loved the world that he gave his only Son, so that everyone who believes in him may not perish but may have eternal life" (John 3:16). In the Greek, however, it isn't really "believes," it is the Greek verb for, "faiths." But we've lost the verb form of the English word "faith," so translators substitute the word "believes." But our relationship isn't grounded in a knowledge of Christian doctrine or any set of beliefs, but in our willingness to entrust our hearts, our lives, our all to Jesus. And not to some pretend-Jesus formed from our imaginations or desires, but the true Jesus, the Jesus-Who-Is. He is the one in whom we must place our trust. Not our 401K or our education or our careers or even our family, but, in the end, simply in Jesus. Will I trust Jesus, truly? That is the question we have to ask ourselves every day, without fail.

Chapter 9

Making Better Choices in Tough Times

Mark 5:24b–34

And a large crowd followed him [Jesus] and pressed in on him. Now there was a woman who had been suffering from hemorrhages for twelve years. She had endured much under many physicians, and had spent all that she had; and she was no better, but rather grew worse. She had heard about Jesus, and came up behind him in the crowd and touched his cloak, for she said, "If I but touch his clothes, I will be made well." Immediately her hemorrhage stopped; and she felt in her body that she was healed of her disease. Immediately aware that power had gone forth from him, Jesus turned about in the crowd and said, "Who touched my clothes?" And his disciples said to him, "You see the crowd pressing in on you; how can you say, 'Who touched me?'" He looked all around to see who had done it. But the woman, knowing what had happened to her, came in fear and trembling, fell down before him, and told him the whole truth. He said to her, "Daughter, your faith has made you well; go in peace, and be healed of your disease."

A Woman Suffers

Sooner or later, we are all personally confronted by suffering. Our suffering might stem from illness or divorce or loss of a job or the death of a loved one. Difficult times come at us from many directions. Suffering, in all its forms, forces us to confront the fact that the world, and our lives in it, are not as they should be. All the brokenness, pain, and strife force us to confront our most foundational beliefs about God and about ourselves. In the midst of difficulty and suffering, do we turn to God or do we turn from God? Such choices are made all the more difficult because pain and hurt and shock often throw us into mental and emotional disarray that can make it hard to think straight or look more than a step or two ahead.

In this story, we meet a woman who has been sick and shunned for twelve years. Mark tells us of the choice she makes.

Jesus has returned to the western shore of the Sea of Galilee. There, he begins to teach but is interrupted by a man named Jairus, an administrator of some sort in the local synagogue, who asks Jesus to come see his dying daughter.[24] While Jesus is making his way to Jairus' home, a large crowd presses in on this miracle worker. In the crowd, there is a woman who has suffered from female hemorrhaging for twelve years. She's been to all the doctors, such as they were in her day, and has spent all her money. She's exhausted her medical alternatives but to no avail. No matter what she's done, she's gotten worse, not better. For twelve years this agony has continued.

As difficult and worrisome as her illness must have been, the nature of her illness rendered her a social outcast. According to Jewish law as set forth by God (see Leviticus 15:25–30), a woman was "unclean" during any time of female hemorrhaging. For most women, this was only several days each month, but for the woman in the crowd, her bleeding means that she has been unclean for twelve years. Any Jew who touches her, or her bed, or anything she has sat upon, would become unclean also; thus, for twelve years this woman has not experienced the slightest touch of another person. It is pretty hard even to imagine what her life must be like. Little wonder that she goes in search of this miracle worker.

A Woman Chooses

Because the woman is ritualistically unclean and untouchable, you can almost picture some people in the crowd struggling to avoid her touch as she surges toward Jesus. Coming up from behind, she touches Jesus' clothing, believing, as do her contemporaries, that Jesus' power would be carried even in his clothing. Though the woman believes that by touching Jesus' clothing she will be healed, in what must be a moment of overwhelming joy, she is healed instantly and feels the overwhelming power of that healing. Jesus too feels the power of the healing, but he is not sure who touched him. He asks his disciples who touched him, but they respond sensibly enough (but with a little exasperation) that it is impossible to know because there are so many people in the crowd. Now, we come to the most amazing part of this story.

This ill and shunned woman, who had found the courage to come to a crowd of people in the first place, and then had been bold enough to touch the miracle-working teacher, now finds the strength to come forward, in all

---

24. The story of the hemorrhaging woman is set in the middle of a larger story about Jesus' raising to life of Jairus' ill daughter.

her fear and trembling, to confess that she was the one who reached out to Jesus. Frankly, it boggles the mind. You and I probably have little appreciation of what it must have taken for her to join the crowd that day in her uncleanness and risk further ostracism. But Jesus understood. When she confesses what she has done (made Jesus ritualistically unclean by touching him), he tells her that her faith has made her well and that she can "go in peace" and be healed of her affliction. The "peace" with which Jesus blesses her is far more than relief from anxiety or fear. This peace is what God wills, not merely for the body or the soul or for the human race, but for his whole creation.[25] This peace is wholeness and salvation. There is a spiritual dimension to Jesus' healing of this woman. Not only does her bleeding stop, but she is made clean, able to touch and be touched. Her steadfast faith in the power of Jesus enables her to begin rebuilding right relationships with her neighbors and loved ones.

Choosing God

The woman had suffered for a very long time. It wouldn't surprise us if she had become bitter and alienated from God. In the midst of suffering, many people do begin to doubt God's love or God's goodness or even God's existence. But this woman did not embrace anger or doubt. She turned to God, not from God. Some might say that her choice was made out of nothing more than blind desperation. Jesus knew otherwise. He saw that her choice to turn to him had been made out of faith alone. Her act of faith resulted in a physical and spiritual healing that went to the center of her being.

God doesn't promise us a physical healing in response to our faith, but he does promise us that he will never abandon us and that, even in the midst of the most profound suffering, we can find wholeness and peace in God's love—if only we will choose to turn to him, not from him.

For a Deeper Understanding

Who Wrote the Gospel of Mark?

Many people do not realize that all four Gospels—Matthew, Mark, Luke, and John—were written anonymously. None of them bear an author's name. These Gospels come to us from the early church, in the first

---

25. G. Kittel and G. Kittel, eds., *Theological Dictionary of the New Testament*, trans. G. W. Bromiley (Grand Rapids, MI: Eerdmans, 1976). The word translated "peace" is *eirene* in the Greek and corresponds to *shalom* in Hebrew.

few centuries after Jesus' resurrection. The early church believed that the writer of Mark's Gospel was a companion of Peter who got most of his material from Peter's preaching and eyewitness accounts. Many early Christians further believed that Mark, the author, was also John Mark in Acts (see Acts 12:2, 25; 15:37–39).

Regardless of who wrote Mark, we, as part of the Christian community, affirm that Mark's Gospel and the rest of the Bible are inspired by God in a way unlike any other writings. We proclaim that all the authors were "illumined by the Holy Spirit" and bear true witness to God and God's work.

A Story Within a Story

At several points in his Gospel, Mark inserts one story into another. The story of the sick woman who touched Jesus' garments is in the middle of a larger story that begins at Mark 5:21.

Jesus has crossed back over the Sea of Galilee. Jairus, an important administrator in the local synagogue, has come pleading that Jesus accompany him to see his dying daughter. The sick woman approaches Jesus while he makes his way to Jairus' home. Before reaching the home, Jesus is told that there is no point in going further for the girl is dead. Jesus replies, "Do not fear, only believe" (v. 36). At Jairus' home people are weeping over the child's death. In contrast to the faith of the hemorrhaging woman, these people scoff at Jesus when he suggests that the girl is not dead, but sleeping. Indeed, Mark tells us that they laugh at Jesus. However, Jesus goes in to see the girl and tells her to "get up" (v. 41)." The twelve-year old immediately gets up, walks around, and begins to eat. These stories make us consider the nature of true faith.

Chapter 10

The Basic Ingredients of Prayer

Matthew 6:5–18

And whenever you pray, do not be like the hypocrites; for they love to stand and pray in the synagogues and at the street corners, so that they may be seen by others. Truly I tell you, they have received their reward. But whenever you pray, go into your room and shut the door and pray to your Father who is in secret; and your Father who sees in secret will reward you. When you are praying, do not heap up empty phrases as the Gentiles do; for they think that they will be heard because of their many words. Do not be like them, for your Father knows what you need before you ask him.

Pray then in this way: Our Father in heaven, hallowed be your name.

Your kingdom come. Your will be done, on earth as it is in heaven.

Give us this day our daily bread. And forgive us our debts, as we also have forgiven our debtors. And do not bring us to the time of trial, but rescue us from the evil one.

For if you forgive others their trespasses, your heavenly Father will also forgive you; but if you do not forgive others, neither will your Father forgive your trespasses. And whenever you fast, do not look dismal, like the hypocrites, for they disfigure their faces so as to show others that they are fasting. Truly I tell you, they have received their reward. But when you fast, put oil on your head and wash your face, so that your fasting may be seen not by others but by your Father who is in secret; and your Father who sees in secret will reward you.

Building a Trusting Relationship

When I began work on this study, I was going to take the Lord's Prayer as a model for our own prayers and then look at some other models or patterns of prayer, such as ACTS (Adoration, Confession, Thanksgiving, Supplication). Such models are helpful, but as I read and re-read Jesus' warnings about hypocrisy and "empty phrases," I came to focus on a deeper meaning of "basic ingredients." What characteristics must be basic to all prayer, and why?

The passage from Matthew is taken from the Sermon on the Mount. Jesus has retreated from the crowds and has gathered his disciples around him. In the very center of this long block of teaching, Jesus turns to the subject of prayer. But before teaching his disciples to pray, Jesus warns them about the basics. They are not to be hypocrites. They are not to pray so that everyone can see what good "pray-ers" they are. When they fast, they ought not to look like they are fasting. They are not to pile up a bunch of empty phrases in their prayers. In all this, Jesus is pushing his disciples toward prayer that is grounded in sincerity and honesty, humility and forgiveness—these are the basic ingredients of prayer that are grounded in true faith! Why?

In the Bible, trust is a synonym for faith. When we say that we have faith in Jesus Christ, we mean that we trust Jesus—completely and utterly. Now, all of us are experienced at building trusting relationships with others, or at least trying to. We know that building trust is not easy. It takes time. We risk trusting a person in small matters so that we might come to trust them in large matters. We know that trust is fragile. Trust takes a long time to build but it can disintegrate in a moment of betrayal. We know that trust must be cherished and protected. And, we know that hypocrisy and empty talk are not the way to build trust.

Prayer is conversation with God—conversation that is to be grounded upon trust. So, just as we strive to be sincere and forthright with those we trust, there can be no hypocrisy or deceit in our prayers to God. The psalmists are sometimes incredibly angry with God and they don't hesitate to voice their anger. Of course, they don't hesitate; they trust God!

Indeed, with God, this is all much easier than it is with any other person we might seek to know and trust. My wife knows me well; we trust each other as much as two people can. But she can't read my mind—though I wonder at times! But God our Father knows what we need before we ask him (v. 8). God's Spirit lifts to God our deepest prayers, even when we can't find the words (Romans 8:26–27).

Prayers Built upon Trust

In the context of this deep, abiding trust in God, Jesus teaches his disciples the Lord's Prayer. He points them toward God's kingdom and teaches them to rely completely on God, even for the daily bread they eat. The disciples are to trust in God's forgiveness, even as they forgive others. Dietrich Bonhoeffer, a modern-day disciple of Jesus Christ who was condemned by the Nazis, was known to pray, "I put my trust in your grace and commit my life wholly in your hands."

Whether we are praising God or thanking him. Whether we are confessing or asking. Whether we come to God with a peaceful heart or an angry one. In all this, we trust that God loves us and hears us and answers us. The basic ingredients of prayer are the same ingredients that build trust between two persons: honesty, sincerity, caring, thanking, appreciating, loving, and serving. Add to this list yourself. And in the end, pray with a trusting heart. Amen.

For a Deeper Understanding

John Calvin 'Going to Work'

John Calvin (1509–1564) was one of the great Protestant reformers. Let's examine two prayers from a collection of everyday prayers Calvin wrote for the people of Geneva, Switzerland. These prayers reflect his conviction that our spiritual faith must be matched with our practical application.

My God, Father and Savior, since you have commanded us to work in order to meet our needs, sanctify our labor that it may bring nourishment to our souls as well as to our bodies. Make us constantly aware that our efforts are worthless unless guided by your light and by your hand. Make us faithful to the particular tasks for which you have bestowed upon us the necessary gifts, taking from us any envy or jealousy at the vocations of others.

Give us a good heart to supply the needs of the poor, saving us from any desire to exalt ourselves over those who receive our bounty. And if you should call us into greater poverty than we humanly desire, save us from any spirit of defiance or resentment, but rather let us graciously and humbly receive the bounty of others. Above all, may every temporal grace be matched by spiritual grace, that in both body and soul we may live to your glory.[26]

---

26.   John Calvin, quoted in John Collins, "A Prayer for Labor Day," *From Behind the Pulpit.* , September 4, 2017, https://revcollins.com/2017/09/04/a-prayer-for-labor-day-2/.

Chapter 10

Dietrich Bonhoeffer "Condemned to Death"

Dietrich Bonhoeffer (1906–1945) was a German Lutheran pastor who publicly opposed the Nazis from 1933 until his execution. In 1943 he was implicated in a plot to assassinate Hitler. Bonhoeffer was jailed by the Nazis and later hung.

O Lord God, Great is the misery that has come upon me. My cares overwhelm me: I am at a loss. O God, comfort and help me. Give me strength to bear what you send, And do not let fear rule over me. As a loving Father, take care of my loved ones, My wife and children. O merciful God, Forgive all the sins I have committed. Against you and against my fellow men. I put my trust in your grace, And commit my life wholly into your hands. Do with me as is best for you, For that will be best for me too. Whether I live or die, I am with you, And you are with me. Lord, I wait for your salvation. And for your kingdom.[27]

---

27.   Dietrich Bonhoeffer, *Letters and Papers from Prison* (London, England: SCM Press, 1953), p.127.

Chapter 11

Secure in the Storm

Psalm 107:28–32
Then they cried to the LORD in their trouble, and he brought them out from their distress; he made the storm be still, and the waves of the sea were hushed. Then they were glad because they had quiet, and he brought them to their desired haven. Let them thank the LORD for his steadfast love, for his wonderful works to humankind. Let them extol him in the congregation of the people, and praise him in the assembly of the elders.

Luke 8:22–25
One day he [Jesus] got into a boat with his disciples, and he said to them, "Let us go across to the other side of the lake." So they put out, and while they were sailing he fell asleep. A windstorm swept down on the lake, and the boat was filling with water, and they were in danger. They went to him and woke him up, shouting, "Master, Master, we are perishing!" And he woke up and rebuked the wind and the raging waves; they ceased, and there was a calm. He said to them, "Where is your faith?" They were afraid and amazed, and said to one another, "Who then is this, that he commands even the winds and the water, and they obey him?"

The Opposite of Faith

Luke tells us a simple yet profound story that begins a new section of his gospel. Luke's story is basically an abridged version of the story as told by Mark (Mark 4:35–41). Jesus has taken some of his disciples on a voyage across the Sea of Galilee, heading for the Gentile lands on the eastern shore. The voyage will take a while; so, not surprisingly, Jesus decides to nap and soon falls asleep. Sudden and violent storms are common on the Sea of Galilee and such a storm quickly engulfs the small craft. The disciples see the boat filling with water and they frantically rush to awaken Jesus, fearing that they may die in the storm. Jesus wakes up, rebukes the storm, and calm returns to the sea. Jesus is disturbed by his disciples' fear, asking them, "Where is your faith?" He knows that fear, not doubt, is the opposite of faith.[28] The disciples were afraid of the storm, but now they are even more afraid.[29] After all, they have just witnessed a power greater than the storm. What did they just witness? "Who then is this?" Who is this man that even storms obey?

Luke has shortened the story told by Mark and driven it quickly to these two questions: "Where is your faith?" and "Who then is this?" We'll take a look at each.

Where Is Your Faith?

Fear and amazement at Jesus' actions were not new to the disciples. Once, Jesus had gone out with them to fish in the Sea of Galilee (Luke 5:1–11) after they had spent a disappointing night on the lake. Jesus instructed them to lower their nets – and the nets were filled to the point of breaking. There were so many fish that the boat threatened to sink under the weight. The disciples were "amazed" (v. 9), but Jesus told them, "Do not be afraid; from now on you will be catching people" (v.11). Peter must have had some inkling of what was going on, for after the miracle he fell at Jesus' knees saying, "Go away from me, Lord, for I am a sinful man!" (v. 8). It is God who cannot abide the presence of sin.

One of the most common questions in my classes is, "Why do the disciples have so much trouble seeing who Jesus is? —why don't they get it?" There is no fully satisfying answer. Preacher Fred Craddock rightly notes that, "They had been with Jesus long enough to have adequate ground for trust in God and in Jesus' access to God's power."[30] Yet, they lose confidence and panick. They are overcome by anxiety because in their own minds and hearts, they are following someone whom they still see as no more than a wise, and very human, teacher. So, it shouldn't surprise us that the disciples seem to be more frightened by Jesus' command of the sea than they are by the storm itself. After all, who could really do such a thing? Even though ancient people ascribed command of the elements to kings and wise men,

---

28. Fred Craddock makes this point in his commentary on Luke. *Luke: Interpretation: A Bible Commentary for Teaching and Preaching* (Louisville, KY: Westminster John Knox Press, 1990).

29. Note that Luke uses the phrase "afraid and amazed" only after Jesus calms the storm. The disciples recognize that such power is the prerogative of God (see Psalms 65:7, 77:16, 89:9, 104:7, 107:23–29; Job 26:12; Jeremiah 5:22). This is from C. Evans' commentary on Luke in the *Word Biblical Commentary* (Grand Rapids, MI: Zondervan, 2002).

30. Craddock. p.115.

in all the ancient Roman, Greek, and Jewish traditions there is no mention of someone who actually did it. But Jesus did. The disciples saw it for themselves.

Who Then Is This?

The Jews were desert people, not seafarers. As New Testament scholar R. Alan Culpepper notes, throughout the Old Testament the sea was depicted as a place of danger. He writes:

> Thus, declarations of God's power over the sea, which often recalled the Exodus, were acclamations of God's power to preserve and protect . . . . By stilling the wind and the waves by his word of command, therefore, Jesus does what in the Old Testament God alone could do. The story is an epiphany, a manifestation of Jesus' divine power and identity.[31]

In Psalm 107, the psalmist praises God for deliverance from stormy seas, confident that God's people could always rest secure in God's arms. This doesn't mean that bad things won't happen to us. Paul was once shipwrecked in a storm, ending up on a deserted beach (Acts 27:9–44). Nonetheless, Paul stayes confident that God's purposes will not be thwarted, that nothing can separate him, or us, from "the love of God in Christ Jesus our Lord," and that "all things work together for good for those who love God" (see Romans 8:28).

For many of us, the storms of life can seem especially intense. The disciples' failure to understand Jesus' identity caused them much needless fear. But we do know Jesus' full identity, that he is both human and divine. We place our faith and trust in Jesus, knowing that in so doing, we find rest and comfort and peace in God's own arms. In Jesus Christ, we find "the peace of God, which surpasses all understanding" (Philippians 4:7). Hallelujah!

For a Deeper Understanding

The Sea of Galilee

The "lake" referred to by Luke is the Sea of Galilee, a harp-shaped body of water about 8 miles across at its widest part. The sea sits astride the Great Rift Valley extending from Egypt upward into Syria. Consequently, the sea is 700 feet below sea level. It is surrounded by steep hills reaching to approximately 1500 ft. The combination of the high hills and low sea causes

---

31. R. Alan Culpepper, "Luke" in *NIB*, vol. 8 (Nashville, TN: Abingdon, 2001), p.184.

abrupt temperature shifts and sudden, violent storms, such as the one that threatened to swamp Jesus and his disciples.

Jesus was raised in Galilee, a hilly region on the western side of the Sea of Galilee. Most of Jesus' public ministry was spent in this area. The Sea of Galilee played an important role in Jesus' life and ministry. Jesus found his first disciples from among men who fished the sea's waters. Further, Jews lived on the western side of the sea, while Gentiles lived on the eastern side. In today's passage, Jesus is crossing the lake to minister among the Gentiles. Jesus' work among Gentiles was always a potent demonstration that the kingdom of God was available to all.

Also, the Bible can be confusing when it comes to names. The Sea of Galilee is also referred to as the Lake of Gennesaret (Luke 5:1), the Sea of Chinnereth (Numbers 34:11), and the Sea of Tiberias (John 6:1). Lands and places would pick up assorted names as maps passed through various hands. Maps in the back of your Bible can help, but even there most maps won't tell you all the names used through the course of biblical history.

Messiah and God

This passage revolves around the question of Jesus' identity. The disciples' faith fails them because they do not understand who Jesus really is. As Luke's gospel presses forward, Jesus confronts the disciples more and more directly. When Jesus asks Peter, "But who do you say that I am?," Peter replies, "The Messiah of God" (Luke 9:20). But even here, Peter does not go far enough. The question of whether Jesus is the Messiah is separate from the question of Jesus' divinity! This is a point of much confusion among Christians. To first-century Jews, Messiah and God were not synonyms. When Peter says that Jesus is the Messiah, he is not claiming that Jesus is God. Rather, Peter is claiming that Jesus is God's agent, the one through whom God will inaugurate his kingdom. Only much later would Jesus' followers come to understand that Jesus is not only fully and truly human, but also fully and truly God.

Chapter 12

Overcoming the Fear of the Unknown

2 Timothy 1:7
For God did not give us a spirit of cowardice,
but rather a spirit of power and of love and of self-discipline.

Numbers 13:30–14:4
But Caleb quieted the people before Moses, and said, "Let us go up at once and occupy it, for we are well able to overcome it." Then the men who had gone up with him said, "We are not able to go up against this people, for they are stronger than we." So they brought to the Israelites an unfavorable report of the land that they had spied out, saying, "The land that we have gone through as spies is a land that devours its inhabitants; and all the people that we saw in it are of great size. There we saw the Nephilim (the Anakites come from the Nephilim); and to ourselves we seemed like grasshoppers, and so we seemed to them." Then all the congregation raised a loud cry, and the people wept that night. And all the Israelites complained against Moses and Aaron; the whole congregation said to them, "Would that we had died in the land of Egypt! Or would that we had died in this wilderness! Why is the LORD bringing us into this land to fall by the sword? Our wives and our little ones will become booty; would it not be better for us to go back to Egypt?" So they said to one another, "Let us choose a captain, and go back to Egypt."

"What Do You Fear?"

Imagine a life without fear, worry, or anxiety. Though God wishes such a life for us, freedom from anxiety often seems beyond our grasp and we must seek to overcome the fears that plague us.

If we stop to think about it, our lives are pretty much one large pile of unknowns. We take risks of one sort or another every day of our lives. Most of these unknowns don't trouble us at all and if they do, we deal with them easily. But sometimes, we face an unknown that terrifies us, paralyzes us, and robs us of whatever peace of mind we might have enjoyed. Such an unknown can cause us to make terrible[32] decisions.

Trust or Turn Back?

This story tells of a choice the Israelites have to make after escaping from slavery in Egypt. After they flee across the Red Sea, God leads Moses and the people to Mt. Sinai where God lays out the covenant with the people on how they will live together. God gives them a set of instructions for what it means to love God and to love their neighbor, including the Ten Commandments. God gives them instructions to build a moveable home in which God will dwell with them. And God leads them from Mt. Sinai to the borders of Canaan so that the Israelites might move into the land that God had promised to Abraham centuries before. Yet despite all this, the people fear the unknown more than they trust God, so an entire generation misses God's promised land. Led astray by the tiny god of their own conception, the people will wander aimlessly for forty years until they die, until their children are ready to trust, fully trust, the God-Who-Is and begin their conquest of Canaan.

Trust or Panic?

Jesus' disciples are faced with big unknowns of their own and, regrettably, their responses are often little better than the Israelites at the borders of Canaan. In the previous chapter, we read the story, as told by Luke, about Jesus and some of his disciples taking a boat across the Sea of Galilee and encountering a surprise storm. In that story, Jesus promptly did two things. First, he "rebuked" the wind and the waves, bringing calm back to the sea.[33] Second, he admonished his disciples for their lack of faith.

The disciples fear the storm because their faith in and their trust of Jesus is weak and feeble. They fear the demonstration of Jesus' authority because they do not really comprehend who it is that they claim to follow. The disciples are like the Israelites who turn back from Canaan, in that the

---

32.   "Terrify," "terror," "terrible," and "terrific" are from the same Latin root, *terribilis*, meaning "to frighten."

33.   Notice that Jesus rebukes the wind and waves. For many of the ancients, demons inhabited the sea, causing storms and other problems. This was especially true for the Jews, for whom the sea was a symbol of chaos and terror. This story is not about Jesus' power over nature, as we often think. This is the story of an exorcism! Hence, the personal "rebuke." Look at Luke 4:39, where Jesus "rebuked" a fever to save Simon's mother-in-law. Surprising stuff.

disciples' conception of Jesus is too small. Their minds and hearts will require some significant expansion if they are to grasp who Jesus really is and trust him enough to set aside all their fears.

A god[34] Too Small

Underlying the fear of the Israelites is their lack of trust that God could actually keep his promises despite the presence of giants in Canaan. Yahweh might be their God, but they ask themselves, is he really more powerful than all the other gods on the block? Jesus might be the disciples' Master and Teacher, but does he really have authority over all creation, including the demons in the sea? These people fear the unknown because their gods are too small.

For a Deeper Understanding

What Is the Opposite of Faith?

The disciples panic during the storm and Jesus scolds them for their lack of faith. We sometimes tend to think that doubt is the opposite of faith, but Craddock[35] and our story in Luke suggest fear is the opposite of faith. Part of our misunderstanding is a language problem.

We translate the Greek word *pistis* as "faith." Regrettably, though, *pistis* has a verb form, while faith does not. No one says, "I faithed yesterday." This is too bad, because Bible translations use "believe" as the verb form of "faith," even though "believe" speaks to a state of mind, including an opinion. Similarly, "doubt" refers to a state of mind. But the best synonym for "faith" is "trust." Faith speaks more to matters of the heart than does belief. It is not so much "what do you think?" as it is "whom do you trust?"

When the disciples panic, it is a lack of trust that leads to their fear. Despite all that they have seen and heard from Jesus, they don't really trust enough to put their lives in Jesus' hands.

---

34. The lower-case "god" is not a typo. In my writing, I reserve "God" to speak of the one true God —the God of Abraham, the God of Israel—Father, Son, and Holy Spirit. All the other supposed gods of this world and of our lives get the lower-case. This approach follows Bible translations such as the NRSV. See Exodus 20:2–3, for example. To get more insight on conquering fear, I recommend J.B. Phillips' *Your God Is Too Small: A Guide for Believers and Skeptics Alike*, a slender volume written more than a half century ago. The book was reissued by Simon & Schuster in 2004.
35. Craddock. p.115.

Chapter 13

Get Out of the Boat!

Matthew 14:22–33
Immediately he made the disciples get into the boat and go on ahead to the other side, while he dismissed the crowds. And after he had dismissed the crowds, he went up the mountain by himself to pray. When evening came, he was there alone, but by this time the boat, battered by the waves, was far from the land, for the wind was against them. And early in the morning he came walking toward them on the sea. But when the disciples saw him walking on the sea, they were terrified, saying, "It is a ghost!" And they cried out in fear. But immediately Jesus spoke to them and said, "Take heart, it is I; do not be afraid." Peter answered him, "Lord, if it is you, command me to come to you on the water." He said, "Come." So, Peter got out of the boat, started walking on the water, and came toward Jesus. But when he noticed the strong wind, he became frightened, and beginning to sink, he cried out, "Lord, save me!" Jesus immediately reached out his hand and caught him, saying to him, "You of little faith, why did you doubt?" When they got into the boat, the wind ceased. And those in the boat worshiped him, saying, "Truly you are the Son of God."

Another Storm

Going to worship each week seems so safe, so comfortable—probably too comfortable. When was the last time any of us took a risk, a big risk, for our faith? Perhaps the skies are darkening as the disciples climb into the boat. Some are experienced fishermen and know how quickly ferocious storms could form over the Sea of Galilee. Perhaps they are even thinking about the time not long before when they had awakened Jesus to save them from a storm (Matthew 8:23– 27). He had, of course, saved them, calming the storm and chastising the disciples for their "little faith" (*oligopistos* in the Greek).

Most likely, the disciples' minds are consumed with what they had just experienced. Just hours before, on a remote shore, Jesus had miraculously fed a huge throng. In front of their own eyes, he had taken five loaves of bread and two fish, looked up to heaven, blessed them, broken the bread, and fed thousands. Then, Jesus had quickly sent the disciples on ahead, instructing them to get into the boat and head out across the sea while he headed into the hills to be alone and to pray.

Jesus had never sent them ahead of him before. He had always been with them, there to protect and to lead. But now they are in the boat alone, heading across the sea in a growing storm. Buffeted by stronger and stronger headwinds, the boat becomes tortured by higher and higher waves. Shortly before dawn, the disciples look out across the sea and see a shocking, and indeed, terrifying sight— Jesus is walking toward them across the surface of the sea.

This story begs us to use our imaginations. Perhaps this is why so much of the Bible contains stories. We can put ourselves in the story in a way that we could never engage an essay on doctrine. Who wouldn't be a little anxious about climbing into the boat without Jesus? There is no indication that Jesus gave the disciples any instruction about what he wanted them to do when they reached the other side of the sea. Who wouldn't be scared as the sea rose and the boat struggled? Who wouldn't be terrified to look over the side of the boat and see someone, anyone, walking on the water? Who might not think it's a ghost or at least a hallucination? Nobody can walk on water—or can they?

Would I respond as Peter does? That is the question. Would I get out of the boat? Peter does. He hears Jesus call out in the wind and identify himself. He hears Jesus tell them all to set aside their fear, to "take heart." Peter yells out that if Jesus calls him, Peter will walk out to him. And when Jesus says, "Come," Peter climbs over the side of the boat. When he gets out there, for at least a few moments Peter walks on the surface of the water himself. But then the wind hits his face. Perhaps he realizes what he is doing. Regardless, he looks toward the storm and away from Jesus—and sinks like a rock. Thrusting his hand upward, Peter crys out, "Save me." And Jesus does. But he also rebukes Peter for his "little faith," *oligopistos*.[36] Pointedly, Jesus asks Peter, "Why did you doubt?"

A Story for the Church

It is not difficult to see why Matthew tells us the story in this way. He is writing to a post-resurrection church that cannot see Jesus and touch

---

36. Matthew would use this word, *oligopistos*, again in the final passage before Peter's confession that Jesus is the Messiah. Matthew only uses the word to describe the weak faith of believers, never unbelievers.

Jesus as the disciples had years before. The disciples had climbed into the boat without Jesus beside them in the same way he always had. They felt alone, but they were not. Jesus was still their Lord, coming to them in the most surprising way. Matthew's community might feel alone, but they aren't alone. Jesus would come to these Christians also, in the most surprising ways.

In response to Jesus' call, Peter climbs out. He responds to Jesus in trust, in faith. But about as soon as he gets out, he takes his eyes off Jesus and sees the storm instead and sinks. Would it have been possible for Peter to have faith so strong that he could walk on water all the way to Jesus? I don't know. All I know is that Peter's faith is fragile, as is my own. It is far too easy, too human, to see the storm and discover that our faith has fled us, replaced by doubts and fears. But Jesus is there to save Peter and is here to save us, to grasp our outstretched hands and pull us to safety. Surely, Matthew wants us to see all this in his telling of the story.

Despite Peter's sinking, notice one thing in the story. Peter does walk on water. He does not climb over the side and slip between the waves. He gets out of the boat and, at least for a moment, walks until he sees the wind. How that moment must have seemed to Peter. When he looks back on it, how does he feel? What thoughts run through his brain? We can't know, but we can know this—if Peter had not gotten out of the boat, he could never have walked on water at all.[37]

Getting Out of the Boat

When Jesus sends the disciples on alone, he knows that he will not always be with them as he is then. He will be with them always in another way, a different way. They will no longer be able to rely on their five senses for their faith in Jesus. They will have to learn that faith is about being certain of what they can't see (Hebrews 11:1). They will have to grow in ways that they can't even imagine at the time.

When Peter steps out of the boat, he takes a risk. It is only by taking a risk that he is able to walk on water at all, if even only for a few moments. We don't often think of our faith as being about risk-taking. We live in a world that makes it seem easy, without risk, to be a Christian—but that is an appealing lie. Being a Christian is risk-free only so long as we don't take it too seriously, don't let our faith truly shape our priorities and agendas. Once we step forward to admit and to proclaim that Jesus is Lord of all creation,

---

37. I highly recommend that you read a book by John Ortberg, *If You Want to Walk on Water, You've Got to Get Out of the Boat* (Nashville, TN: Zondervan, 2014).

much less of our own lives, we embark on a journey that is all about taking risks, about stepping out of the boat ourselves.

For a Deeper Understanding

The Purpose of Matthew's Gospel

Anyone who writes anything does so with a purpose. It might be to inform or to persuade. It might be to get a good grade or create a record of what happened. Every writer brings not only a purpose, but a point of view. This is no less true of the Gospel writers than it is any other author. Scripture is, to use Paul's phrase, "God-breathed," but it is also the work of human authors. Thus, an important question is, "What can we know about Matthew's purpose in writing?"

Matthew was Jewish and he wrote for a Jewish audience, which explains the lengthy Jewish genealogy that opens his Gospel. Matthew wrote his gospel late in his own life, forty or more years after Jesus' death and resurrection in 30 AD. Matthew had Mark's Gospel to work from, in addition to his own recollections and other sources. At times, Matthew copied Mark word-for-word, but at other times modified Mark's account, as in today's story. Why did Matthew include Peter's stepping out of the boat when Mark did not?

It seems virtually certain that Matthew wrote for a community of Jewish Christians. He went so far as to avoid the phrase, "kingdom of heaven," for fear that the word "God" might offend those Jews who would not utter God's name in any form. Instead, Matthew uses "kingdom of heaven." He painstakingly portrays Jesus as the fulfillment of Jewish messianic prophecies and expectations.

When we read a story like this one, we can be comforted knowing that it was written to bolster the faith of Christians who struggled with doubts and fears just like our own. Matthew told the story in this way so that his community would be strengthened in their faith, so that they would understand who it was they worshipped. Matthew wanted them to take risks, to step out of the boat, and to keep their eyes focused upon Jesus.

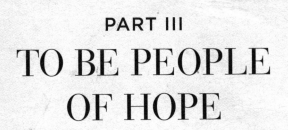

PART III

TO BE PEOPLE
OF HOPE

Hope is a tricky word. The world uses it one way; believers use it in a different way. The world hopes to win the game or the lottery, to overcome an illness or get a better job. But in the Church, the body of Christ, hope means something else. Our hope is our sure and certain confidence that, in the end, all will be well and that we and all creation will be renewed and restored by God. It is a hope anchored in the knowledge that, truly, Jesus was resurrected almost two millennia ago. It is a hope birthed by God's love. As I heard a few days ago, God doesn't promise a better tomorrow; God offers us eternity. When times are tough as they too often are, for us all, we turn to the truth of God's love revealed on a cross and know that, " . . . neither death, nor life, nor angels, nor rulers, nor things present, nor things to come, nor powers, nor height, nor depth, nor anything else in all creation, will be able to separate us from the love of God in Christ Jesus our Lord" (Romans 8:38–39).

Thirsting for God?

Psalm 34:1–8; 17–19 (MSG)
I bless GOD every chance I get; my lungs expand with his praise.
I live and breathe GOD; if things aren't going well, hear this and be happy:
Join me in spreading the news; together let's get the word out.
GOD met me more than halfway, he freed me from my anxious fears.
Look at him; give him your warmest smile. Never hide your feelings from him.
When I was desperate, I called out, and GOD got me out of a tight spot.
GOD's angel sets up a circle of protection around us while we pray.
Open your mouth and taste, open your eyes and see—how good GOD is.
Blessed are you who run to him.
Is anyone crying for help? GOD is listening, ready to rescue you. If your heart
is broken, you'll find GOD right there; if you're kicked in the gut, he'll help
you catch your breath.
Disciples so often get into trouble; still, GOD is there every time.

Psalm 63:1–8
O God, you are my God, I seek you, my soul thirsts for you; my flesh faints
for you, as in a dry and weary land where there is no water. So, I have looked
upon you in the sanctuary, beholding your power and glory. Because your
steadfast love is better than life, my lips will praise you. So, I will bless you
as long as I live; I will lift up my hands and call on your name. My soul is
satisfied as with a rich feast, and my mouth praises you with joyful lips when
I think of you on my bed and meditate on you in the watches of the night; for
you have been my help, and in the shadow of your wings I sing for joy. My soul
clings to you; your right hand upholds me.

The Holy Habit of Prayer

Do you thirst for God? Do you live and breathe God? If your answers
are yes, then the holy habit of prayer will be as natural as eating or drinking.
If your answer is no, then the holy habit of prayer must become part of your
path to such joyful thirst.

In Psalm 63, the psalmist stands with open mouth, thirsting for God, hungering for God, praying to God, praising God. He thinks about God at night, in the dark. The psalmist's soul clings to God like a child that clings to its mother. The psalmist lifts up his hands to God, calls God by name, and trusts God. What a powerful image of someone who has given themselves over to God completely, holding nothing back. Someone who has dropped all pretensions to self-sufficiency. Someone who has transcended the world's appetites.

Likewise, with Psalm 34: Living and breathing God! "Open your mouth and taste...how good God is." No wonder the psalmist can't wait to get the word out. He has found his true home and met the God who has always been there.

Do the psalmists describe your own relationship with God? For what or whom do you hunger? What do you think about at night? For many Christians, these images can be a bit intimidating or at least very "other"— certainly not describing themselves. The world seeks to cultivate very different appetites in us and often succeeds.

Yet, such joyful thirsting and fulfillment is not some impossible ideal nor the privilege of a special few. Rather, it is available to us all. God desires it for us all. It is this for which we were made and for which our souls long.

Prayer, one of the long-practiced spiritual disciplines, is necessary to our spiritual growth, to becoming people who live and breathe God. Still, for many of us, the question is where do we begin?

How To Pray (And How Not To)

Though prayer consists of more than our words, setting aside time for deliberate prayer is important, even essential. Here are a few tips that many Christians have found helpful as they work toward a deeper prayer life:

- Don't just think the words—say them. A wandering mind is one of the biggest hurdles to a rich prayer life and it happens to all of us. Actually speaking the prayer will help you stay on track.

- Don't just pray about what you'd like God to do. Tell God how you feel. Make time to give thanks and even to be honest with God about your mistakes or failures. Try to be specific in your prayers.

- Keep a prayer list. Most of us have trouble remembering everything on the fly.

- Pray in this way daily—and don't be afraid to start small. Even five minutes a day is a good start. Too many people never start because they intimidate themselves right from the beginning.

- Say grace before each meal. This seems like such a small thing, but you'll find that it helps you to stay more aware of God all day. If the setting is inappropriate for you to pray aloud, even a silent word of grace will be meaningful.

For a Deeper Understanding

What Is Prayer?

We pray when we plead to God for help in times of need. We pray when we thank God for all we have and enjoy. We pray when we praise God. We pray when we reveal to God our concerns for others. We pray when we pause to reflect upon the deep love that God has for us all. We pray when we offer our own love to God.

In his book Prayer, Richard Foster writes about 21 forms of prayer.[38] But even Foster does not exhaust prayer's meaning. Prayer is all this and more.

It is very easy for us to fall into the trap of thinking that prayer consists only of the words spoken to God. But Paul can urge the Thessalonians to "pray without ceasing" because he knows that prayer is not a paragraph but a life. When we live with God at the center of all we do, when we live in oneness with Jesus Christ, we are living a life of prayer, a life of constant conversation with God. Sometimes this conversation is spoken aloud (at least on our end!). Sometimes this conversation is spoken in silence. And sometimes this conversation is only felt. Indeed, there are times when God carries us in this conversation. Paul wrote this to the Christians in Rome: "And the Holy Spirit helps us in our distress. For we don't even know what we should pray for, nor how we should pray. But the Holy Spirit prays for us with groanings that cannot be expressed in words. And the Father who knows all hearts knows what the Spirit is saying, for the Spirit pleads for us believers in harmony with God's own will" (Romans 8:26–27, Author's Translation).

Does God Answer Prayer?

Of course!! What sort of loving father ignores his children? Jesus repeatedly teaches his disciples (that includes us!) that we can rely on God in all things. Now, we may not always get the answer to our prayers that we

---

38.   Richard J. Foster, Prayer: Finding the Heart's True Home (New York, NY: Harper Collins, 2002).

want nor when we want it. After all, the parent often knows better than the child what is best for the child.

In the same way, God knows our hearts and needs better than we do. With boldness, the psalmist writes, "But truly God has listened; he has given heed to the words of my prayer" (Psalm 66:19). The only question for us is whether we will trust God. Will we trust that he listens and answers, even when it seems to us that he does not?

Can Prayer Change God's Mind?

I will always remember what I was once told by a young woman. She said that of all the things we Christians claim are true, the most difficult one for her to believe was that God heard her prayers. The Creator and Sustainer of the Cosmos listening to the words of one young woman? It is hard to believe! But, of course, no harder than that this same God became flesh and was born to another young woman.

Many Christians struggle with prayer. I believe that one of the reasons, perhaps the biggest one, is that we have notions about God that undermine our confidence in God. I see this in the questions I get about prayer: Doesn't God know what I'm going to pray before I do? What good will it do? Isn't the future already set? If not, how could we say God knows the future? How can prayer actually change anything?

The Bible often paints a portrait of God that is a good bit different from what many of us carry around in our heads. For example, Abraham negotiates with God over the fate of Sodom and Gomorrah. Negotiates?? I'm sure Plato and Aristotle never imagined anyone negotiating with the Unmoved Mover. In the second story, Jacob physically wrestles with God on a riverbank. Wrestles with God? Despite the puzzling strangeness of these stories and others like them, I believe they convey deep truths about the nature of God—and it doesn't sound much like Plato.

Here is another story that will make you stop and think. It is from 2 Kings 20. Hezekiah is the king of Judah at the time when the Assyrians are the great power in the region and have overrun the nation of Israel to Judah's north. The Assyrians seems poised to overrun Judah and Jerusalem as well. Indeed, it seems inevitable. Instead, Hezekiah prays for Jerusalem's deliverance. Then, Isaiah prophesies that the city will be saved and God does just that. An angel defeats the Assyrian army as they sleep (see 2 Kings 17–19 for all this).

King Hezekiah is one of the few Israelite kings to get a good report card in Scripture. Most of the kings, like Ahab, do what was evil in God's sight but Hezekiah does "what was right in the sight of the LORD" (2 Kings 18:3). He is even compared to David!

At one point, Hezekiah falls ill. The prophet Isaiah shows up and brings Hezekiah this word from God: "Put your house in order, because you are going to die; you will not recover" 2 Kings 20:1 NIV). Isaiah turns to make his way out of the palace. But Hezekiah turns his face to the wall andbegins to pray: "'Remember, LORD, how I have walked before you faithfully and with wholehearted devotion and have done what is good in your eyes.' And Hezekiah wept bitterly" (20:3 NIV).

Before Isaiah is even able to get out of the palace, the "word of the LORD came to him" (20:4). Isaiah is to turn around and go back to Hezekiah to tell him, The LORD..says: I have heard your prayer and seen your tears; I will heal you . . . I will add fifteen years to your life" (20:5-6 NIV).

What are we are supposed to do with this story? Either God isn't truthful when he tells Hezekiah that the king will soon die, which can't be right, or Isaiah gets it all wrong, which undermines the Bible, or—God changes his mind in response to prayer. But how can God change his mind? Does that idea even make any sense if God knows not only the past and present, but also the future? If we take Scripture seriously, as being "God-breathed" (2 Timothy 3:16 NIV), then this story, like the stories about Abraham's negotiation and Jacob's wrestling match, has to be taken seriously. Could it be that we matter so much to God, that the Creator of the Cosmos not only hears us, but responds to us, even changing his plans? Could our prayers really matter that much? If more of us believed that prayers really do matter, fewer of us would struggle with our prayer lives. In fact, you might hardly be able to shut us up!

Chapter 15

Betting on the Future

Jeremiah 32:6–15 (MSG)
Jeremiah said, "GOD's Message came to me like this: Prepare yourself! Hanamel, your uncle Shallum's son, is on his way to see you. He is going to say, 'Buy my field in Anathoth. You have the legal right to buy it.' And sure enough, just as GOD had said, my cousin Hanamel came to me while I was in jail and said, 'Buy my field in Anathoth in the territory of Benjamin, for you have the legal right to keep it in the family. Buy it. Take it over.'

That did it. I knew it was GOD's Message.

So I bought the field at Anathoth from my cousin Hanamel. I paid him seventeen silver shekels. I followed all the proper procedures: In the presence of witnesses, I wrote out the bill of sale, sealed it, and weighed out the money on the scales. Then I took the deed of purchase— the sealed copy that contained the contract and its conditions and also the open copy—and gave them to Baruch son of Neriah, the son of Mahseiah. All this took place in the presence of my cousin Hanamel and the witnesses who had signed the deed, as the Jews who were at the jail that day looked on.

Then, in front of all of them, I told Baruch, 'These are orders from GOD-of-the-Angel-Armies, the God of Israel: Take these documents—both the sealed and the open deeds—and put them for safekeeping in a pottery jar. For GOD-of-the-Angel-Armies, the God of Israel, says, "Life is going to return to normal. Homes and fields and vineyards are again going to be bought in this country."

Coming Destruction?

Uncertainties about the future threaten to overwhelm us at times. Are we willing to invest for tomorrow? To bet on the future? Jeremiah places a bet that the future is God's. Are we as confident of God and as trusting that, in the end, we are in God's hands?

A few years ago, *Early Edition* was a popular television series. It told the story of a young man who was visited daily by a yellow cat delivering a copy of tomorrow's paper, sending the hero on a mission to prevent a pending tragedy that the "early edition" revealed.

I guess as a metaphor, Jeremiah is the cat. Both in word and deed, Jeremiah brings God's message about Jerusalem's coming destruction. Jeremiah brings this message to God's people in what he says and, more so than any other prophet, in what he does. But whereas the cat turned the message over to someone ready to do something about it, Jeremiah's message goes unheeded. By the time we get to today's Scripture passage in Jeremiah, the Babylonian army has besieged the city. By this time, it doesn't take a magical cat or a prophet of God for everyone to know what comes next—devastation and exile.

The Book of Consolation

We know Jeremiah better than we do any other of the Old Testament prophets. The other prophets' work consists largely of bringing God's messages to the people. The prophets are speakers of God's words. But with Jeremiah, God goes further. Jeremiah not only brings God's messages, but he is also told to enact God's messages in dramatic demonstrations. For example, God tells Jeremiah to stand in front of the temple and proclaim judgment upon the temple (Ch. 7). Jeremiah is told to wear a loincloth and then bury it in some rocks, where it is ruined, symbolizing the relationship between the people and God—once as close as we wear clothing and now in ruins (Ch. 13). Jeremiah is not to take a wife, for God has been cheated upon by his "wife," his people (Ch. 16). Jeremiah is sent to a potter's house to see pottery destroyed (Ch. 18). He smashes an earthenware jug, just as Judah is about to be smashed (Ch. 19).

After all this and more, we are relieved when we get to Chapters 30-33, for these are often called Jeremiah's little book of consolation. These four chapters express a message of hope and restoration. That after all the destruction and exile, God will restore the people to their own land and to freedom.[39] In his commentary on Jeremiah, Old Testament scholar R. E. Clements writes:

---

39. It is promises such as these that create so much tension by Jesus' day. For by then, the Jews, though back on the land, would have spent centuries trading one foreign oppressor for another. Thus, many first-century Jews asked when God would finally keep all these promises. When would the true exile end? For Christians, Jesus is the fulfillment of these promises and the bringer of the new covenant promised by God in Jeremiah 31:31–33. This is a covenant written on the heart, not on tablets of stone.

Beyond the judgments which have taken place, therefore, the Book of Jeremiah asserts categorically that hope remained real: After all that had occurred in bringing ruin and devastation to Judah, there would be divine restoration. The twin themes of return and restoration to a full national existence provide the essential content of the prophetic message of hope, and this message is substantially the same in all four of the great prophetic collections. Eventually and certainly Israel would be saved (30:7); and this word of hope contains an implied assumption that salvation would consist of Israel's becoming a nation once again, free from all the restraints and impositions of foreign rule. Israel would become free, prosperous, and honored under the just government of a Davidic king (cf. 33:19–26).[40]

Sure, I'll Take That Bet[41]

In the above passage, Jeremiah is given another symbolic action to accomplish. With the Babylonian army arrayed outside the walls of Jerusalem, God tells Jeremiah to go out and buy a plot of land in his hometown of Anathoth, about three miles northeast of Jerusalem.[42] What is going through Jeremiah's mind? This must seem as idiotic to him as it does to anyone else. The death of Israel is at hand and Jeremiah is supposed to go make a land investment. Five times in this brief passage, Jeremiah makes it clear that this is God's doing, saying "Thus says the LORD." Based on all the other stuff God has told him to do, Jeremiah probably figures that the land will be lost, just as the loincloth is ruined and the earthenware jug broken.

But instead, v. 15 makes clear that this time, the action is not an enactment of loss but of hope. God is having Jeremiah buy the land for the future, the day when the Israelites will return to Judah. Jeremiah is going to make a profit on this field of hope.

Notice also the care that is paid to the details in this story. There are witnesses, the money is weighed, the deed carefully preserved. This is a symbolic act, but it is also quite real. Jeremiah is putting real money on the line. He is not just standing on the promises of God, he is betting on them!

---

40.   R. E. Clements, *Jeremiah: Interpretation: A Bible Commentary for Teaching and Preaching.* (Louisville, KY: Westminster John Knox Press, 1998). p.175.

41.   Anthony Saldarini's reflections on this passage are very helpful. His commentary is part of *The New Interpreter's Bible*, the twelve-volume edition that is in many church and public libraries.

42.   Since Anathoth was a few miles from Jerusalem, Jeremiah would have had to go and buy the land during one of the occasional respites from the lengthy siege warfare of Nebuchadnezzar.

Jeremiah is investing in the future, but it is not merely educated guess-work. Jeremiah's bet is an act of trust and hope. There is risk to it. Jeremiah may be God's prophet, but he is still a man, still one of us, subject to the same fears and uncertainties as all humans. If you doubt this, just picture Jesus in the Garden of Gethsemane. Even our Lord and Savior is not im-mune to fear.

But regardless of how risky this investment might have seemed to him, Jeremiah lays out the money because his hope rests on his confidence in the promises of God. His hope and our own is not a matter of mere wishes or carefully calculated probabilities. Our hope lies in our confidence that God is faithful.

For a Deeper Understanding

Exile!

It is probably difficult for us to grasp the shock of exile. Sometime around 800 BC, the Greek epic poet Homer wrote, "for there is nothing dearer to a man than his own country and his parents, and however splen-did a home he may have in a foreign country, if it be far from father or mother, he does not care about it." We live in a very mobile society. Corpo-rate moves are a staple of our lives. Somehow, we must emotionally connect with the ancient Israelites and the depth of their despair.

Just imagine: you are a member of the house of Judah, living in Jeru-salem. God, the LORD, the creator of everything, has chosen you to be his people! And he has given you the land of Canaan. He has given you a king, having promised centuries before that someone from the house of David will forever sit on the throne of Israel. But now, the hated Babylonians are running through the streets of Jerusalem. In the distance, you see the tem-ple burning. In your heart, you know that the most sacred of all objects in Israel, the Ark of the Covenant, is lost. Surely, the pagans will simply carry it off and melt it down. You harbor the hope that God will come riding in at the last minute to save you—again. But not this time. Instead, soldiers ap-pear at your door, ordering you and your family to join the caravans headed into exile in Babylonia. As you leave Jerusalem, you see that only the poor-est of families are left behind. The city lies in ruin and death hangs in the air.

It is in the face of such devastation that God tells Jeremiah to buy the plot of land, to make a bet on the future.

A Helping Hand

1 Peter 2:11–17; 3:7–11

Beloved, I urge you as aliens and exiles to abstain from the desires of the flesh that wage war against the soul. Conduct yourselves honorably among the Gentiles, so that, though they malign you as evildoers, they may see your honorable deeds and glorify God when he comes to judge. For the Lord's sake accept the authority of every human institution, whether of the emperor as supreme, or of governors, as sent by him to punish those who do wrong and to praise those who do right. For it is God's will that by doing right you should silence the ignorance of the foolish. As servants of God, live as free people, yet do not use your freedom as a pretext for evil. Honor everyone. Love the family of believers. Fear God. Honor the emperor.

Husbands, in the same way, show consideration for your wives in your life together, paying honor to the woman as the weaker sex, since they too are also heirs of the gracious gift of life—so that nothing may hinder your prayers. Finally, all of you, have unity of spirit, sympathy, love for one another, a tender heart, and a humble mind. Do not repay evil for evil or abuse for abuse; but, on the contrary, repay with a blessing. It is for this that you were called—that you might inherit a blessing. For "Those who desire life and desire to see good days, let them keep their tongues from evil and their lips from speaking deceit; let them turn away from evil and do good; let them seek peace and pursue it."

Living among and with Others

Today's first passage begins a lengthy section of Peter's letter, 2:11–4:11, that focuses on how these believers are to live in the midst of indifference and even outright hostility that has led to their alienation and suffering. Should they isolate themselves and build fences within which they can strive to live the Jesus way? Should they march out ready to do battle, at least figuratively, with all who oppose them or have caused them pain and loss?

It is easy to turn inward when things get tough, when we feel pressed in upon from all sides. In his letter of encouragement, Peter begins to turn our attention outward. In this passage, Peter turns the believers toward others, not only their families and households, but to all those among whom they live.

Preacher and scholar David Bartlett highlights two ways these passages are often read. One reading is that these believers are genuine outcasts from society and that their concern was to form a strong group identity:

> John H. Elliott, in his book *A Home for the Homeless*, has maintained that the Christians who received this letter were sociologically, and not only spiritually, sojourners and exiles. They were among the marginalized people of Asia Minor, living at the edges of power and prestige. As Christians, too, these believers were divorced from acceptable communities of belief and authority. In sociological terms, the Christians who first read 1 Peter were part of a sectarian movement. As with sects in our own time, argues Elliott, one of their concerns was to form a strong group identity, and the way in which they did that was to adopt standards for the ethical life that set them apart from their non-Christian neighbors.
>
> For the Christian community, in other words, there exists a different standard of values, namely the will of God and the exemplary obedience of Jesus Christ, which distinguishes it from outside society. In the estimation of the Gentiles the Christians amount only to a motley collection of lowly aliens, ignoble slaves, religious fanatics and "Christ-lackeys" obsessed with self-humiliation. Within the family of God, however, and in God's estimation, Christians enjoy a new status which can only be retained by avoiding conformity to the degrading social norms of the Gentiles.... Over against the futile world of the Gentiles the Christians constitute an alternative and superior form of social and religious organization.[43]

On the other hand, it is possible to look at Peter's "household code" and hear Peter urging these believers to live virtuously as an example to those who persecute them.

Bartlett rightly notes that these communities probably embraced both perspectives. We sometimes sum this dilemma up with a phrase like, "be in the world but not of the world." We, like these Christians in Asia Minor, can't very well just withdraw from the world. Jesus tells us to go to the ends of the earth and make disciples. "You are the light of the world," (Matthew 5:14) Jesus tells his disciples. "Let your light shine before others . . . ." (Matthew 5:16)

No, we can't withdraw from the world, even when tough times might make us feel like we want to. We are to be a witness to others, honoring

---

43. David L. Bartlett, "1st Peter," in *NIB*, vol. 12 (Nashville, TN: Abingdon, 1998), p.270.

God in all that we do. We are to be honorable people of a "tender heart and a humble mind," even as we strive to preserve and to grow not only our families but the body of Christ.

Thus, Peter tells the husbands that they are to honor their wives. The women who are married to unbelievers are to remind themselves that the "purity and reverence" (1 Peter 3:2) of their lives may win their husbands over to Christ. Slaves are to accept their masters' authority, even that of masters who are harsh.[44] If they or, for that matter, any believer suffers, they at least know that Christ suffered for them. All are to honor everyone, even the emperor!

In all their relationships, perhaps especially so amidst the tensions and stresses of hardship, the believers are to "have unity of spirit, sympathy, love for one another, a tender heart, and a humble mind."

"Doing Good"

In 3:10–11, Peter draws on Psalm 34:12–16 to help the believers see better the shape of this life to which they have been called and which will sustain them through their present hardships. Eugene H. Peterson paraphrases the psalmist's words this way: "Turn your back on sin, do something good; Embrace peace—don't let it get away!" (Psalm 34:14 MSG).

As I reflected on this passage and my own "desire to see good days," as Peter puts it, I was drawn to the simple encouragement to do something good. And having survived tough times in my life, I know well that it is tempting to withdraw from the world, to crawl into a corner and lick my wounds.

But Christ calls us to reach out to others, to family and friends, even to strangers. Reach out not so much looking for help, but seeking to provide help. Tough times challenge us to get outside ourselves, to see that there are those who desperately need our help.

For a Deeper Understanding

The Weaker Sex?

There are some (no, many) places in Scripture, such as 1 Peter 3:7, that slap us upside the head, forcing us to remember that these are the writings

---

44.   Again, verses such as this fall hard on ears and on our hearts. The choice is either to ignore them, pretending they are not there, or try to read them within their historical context and strive to discern meaning for ourselves. The fact that these sorts of verses were horrifyingly misused to justify slavery in America shouldn't blind us to the fact that even here, God may have a message for you and for me.

of people who lived thousands of years ago. They don't share all our values and sensibilities. Their worldviews, even those of the apostles, varied considerably from our own.

For example, it is difficult for me to really imagine that there was a time when slavery was not only acceptable, but understood to be the "natural" order of things. Paul and Peter lived in such a world. Neither advocated the end of slavery. I doubt either of them envisioned a world without slavery, short of the world's remaking at the time of Christ's return. They both had much to say about what it meant to be a Christian slave-owner or a Christian slave. The abolition of the institution would take the better part of two millennia. Yet, when the movement began, it was begun by Christians.

This same unquestioning of culture applies to the place of women in the ancient world. The cultures were patriarchal. Women were poorly educated and expected to largely stay in the private arena of the home. They simply were not seen as being as capable or strong or trustworthy as men. Women couldn't even testify in a Jewish court of law. When you meet a woman in the Bible who has an active and public life, you can bet that you are meeting a formidable person. I once heard a lecture by a scholar on ancient Greece and Rome entitled: "Less Than Human: Women and Slaves in the Greco-Roman World." From the title, you can get the lecturer's point.

Here's another illustration of my point. Dan Brown's famous novel, *The Da Vinci Code*, is built in part on a foundation of the Gnostic writings of the second through fourth centuries, the most well-known of which is the Gospel of Thomas, a second-century writing. At the end of the list of Jesus' secret sayings, Jesus tells Peter that he is going to make Mary Magdalene a male so she can be a "living spirit" like the rest of the guys. Jesus says, "For every female who makes herself male will enter heaven's kingdom." The Gnostics, you see, seemed to believe that females were males whose development had been stunted and thus needed to complete their growth to full, kingdom-ready, personhood.

Needless to say, we need to let ourselves be a bit pleasantly surprised whenever the apostles lift a woman to a prominent place in the movement, such as Lydia, Phoebe, Priscilla, and Junia. We need to cheer when Paul writes that in Christ, "There is no longer Jew or Greek, there is no longer slave or free, there is no longer male and female; for all of you are one in Christ Jesus" (Galatians 3:28).

Seek Peace and Pursue It

Peace so often eludes us. We find ourselves to be anxious and uncertain, unsure of where to turn next or how to go about finding the life we seek. The ancient Jews understood that the peace we seek can be found only in our relationship with God. They had a word for this: *shalom*. It cannot be translated into English with a single word. *Shalom* is prosperity, health, peace, wellness, completeness, safety, harmony, satisfaction, fulfillment, unity, victory, and restoration.

Though we usually think of peace in the sense of our own inner peace, *shalom* for the ancient Jews was often a relational word, nearly synonymous with justice. It was about two persons living in an equitable, often covenantal, relationship. Thus, in the Old Testament, *shalom* can come when a payment is made or an obligation is met, for equity is restored between the two parties. Payment of the tithe, what was to be returned to God, was crucial to maintaining the Israelites' covenantal relationship with YHWH.

Simply put, *shalom* is the restoration of wholeness. It is well-being and is bound up with our relationship with God. Only when we love God and love neighbor, which is the heart of that relationship and which is grounded in action, can we find the peace we seek and that God desires for us.

But we cannot expect to find this peace so long as we hold back any portion of ourselves or our life, as if what matters is only our time or only our talents or only our money. And it won't come if we give from the leftovers, rather than from the first fruits of our lives and work. The wholeness that is *shalom* is just that, encompassing all that we are and have, holding nothing back.

Those Troublesome Household Codes

These passages from 1 Peter resemble what the ancients knew as a "household code." These codes were advice and instruction on how the members of households were to conduct themselves. Peter's here is brief, but Paul has several in his letters and they are often lengthy. We'll take a quick look at Paul's to get a better understanding of these codes among the believers.

Household codes were common in the ancient world. They outlined duties and responsibilities for the management of one's private affairs. What is most striking about Paul's codes is that for every instruction Paul gives the wife or the children, he's got four instructions for the husband. Why? Because the greatest challenges posed by the Christian life fell on the husband.

In the Greco-Roman world of Paul's day, the male head of household was all-powerful, the paterfamilias, the head of the family. According to Roman law, the paterfamilias even had the power to decide whether newborn infants should live or die. For Paul to tell the paterfamilias that he is to love and cherish his wife and family as Christ loved and cherished the church—well, I bet that went down hard. Sacrificial love would not have been the modus operandi of most Greco-Roman husbands. Actually, doing as Paul instructs would require the paterfamilias to set aside willingly all the privileges and prerogatives accorded him by Roman law and social norms.

Paul uses the word submit now and then in his codes, conjuring up words like "subordinate" and "sub-par." How do we handle Paul's instructions written to a world so different from our own? What would Paul say to husbands and wives today?

Unquestionably, Paul lived and wrote within a patriarchal world which often saw women as inferior. Further, the Greek word that Paul uses clearly implies a hierarchy of authority. But if this is all we hear, we miss Paul's dramatic reshaping of marriage relationships among the believers.

In his ministry, Paul does not seek to overthrow the social structures that dominated the ancient world. Paul never advocates the end of slavery. Slavery was a "given" in the ancient world. Likewise, Paul can't conceive of a world in which wives do not defer to their husbands. But Paul does challenge these new Christians' beliefs about the proper exercise of authority and the meaning of power. Indeed, we see this in the responsibilities he gives to women in his ministry, such as to Phoebe and to Priscilla.

Marriage is an example of how Paul understands the cross to have reshaped relationships within households. For Paul, husbands are to take the lead in the marriage and in the household, but their model for what this means is Jesus Christ. And for Paul to speak of Christ is to speak of the cross, of Jesus' loving sacrifice for others. Yes, Paul writes, husbands are to take the lead but there is never room for arrogance, bullying, or abuse. They are to love their wives sacrificially and faithfully, just as Jesus loves his people.

Chapter 17

A Mercy Received

1 Peter 2:1–10

Rid yourselves, therefore, of all malice, and all guile, insincerity, envy, and all slander. Like newborn infants, long for the pure, spiritual milk, so that by it you may grow into salvation—if indeed you have tasted that the Lord is good. Come to him, a living stone, though rejected by mortals yet chosen and precious in God's sight, and like living stones, let yourselves be built into a spiritual house, to be a holy priesthood, to offer spiritual sacrifices acceptable to God through Jesus Christ. For it stands in scripture: "See, I am laying in Zion a stone, a cornerstone chosen and precious; and whoever believes in him will not be put to shame." To you then who believe, he is precious; but for those who do not believe, "The stone that the builders rejected has become the very head of the corner," and "A stone that makes them stumble, and a rock that makes them fall." They stumble because they disobey the word, as they were destined to do. But you are a chosen race, a royal priesthood, a holy nation, God's own people, in order that you may proclaim the mighty acts of him who called you out of darkness into his marvelous light. Once you were not a people, but now you are God's people; once you had not received mercy, but now you have received mercy."

A Letter of Encouragement in Tough Times

In tough times, it helps to be reminded of our larger purpose, why it is that God has called us to him. None of us has a small part to play in God's rescue work. 1 Peter is a letter of encouragement in tough times, written to believers in Asia Minor who now live on "the margins of respectable society" and who have "become victims of social ostracism, their allegiance to Christ having won for them slander, animosity, reproach, scorn, vilification, and contempt."[45] These Christians are paying a steep social, economic, and personal price for placing their faith in Jesus Christ.

What sort of letter would you write? What would you say to them? Peter begins his letter by reminding them of God's great mercy. The believers have been given "a new birth into a living hope" (1 Peter 1:3) and "into an inheritance that is imperishable, undefiled, and unfading." (1 Peter 1:4). The joy of salvation is theirs, Peter writes. Then, Peter urges them to live disciplined and holy lives, perhaps knowing that in times of stress, anxiety, and fear it is often God who goes first, pushed aside by the crises of the moment.

In this passage, Peter calls on these believers to long for spiritual nourishment and embrace their new identity as God's chosen and holy people, knowing always why God has called them to his family.

God's People, a Holy People

Peter writes to Christians who feel like aliens and exiles in their own lands. Echoing God's word brought by Moses, Peter encourages them by reminding them of their place among God's people. Like the ancient Israelites, these Christians are a "royal priesthood" and a "holy nation" upon whom worldly power and holy purpose converge.[46] They have been called out of the darkness for a reason, a purpose. Peter states this purpose simply: Christians are to proclaim God's mighty acts.

What kind of people does it take to proclaim God's mighty acts, to build for God's kingdom?

New Testament scholar Eugene Boring identifies five imperatives for the believers in Peter's first and second chapters.

1. Live in the hope of Christ's return;
2. Be holy, living a life set apart for God's service;
3. Live in reverent fear[47] of God, rather than living for the oppressive culture in which they find themselves;

---

45. Paul J. Achtemeier, Joel B. Green, and Marianne Meye Thompson, *Introducing the New Testament: Its Literature and Theology* (Grand Rapids, MI: Eerdmans, 2001).

46. Not only are there many direct quotations of the Old Testament in the New Testament, there are countless allusions and echoes. When Peter calls the believers a "holy nation" it is a loud echo of Exodus 19:5-6, but there is a very important difference. Moses brings a promise from God that is conditional: "If you obey my voice and keep my covenant . . . you shall be for me a priestly kingdom and a holy nation . . . ." In contrast, Peter simply states a fact: "You are a chosen race, a royal priesthood, a holy nation . . . ." The covenant-keeping has been done for us by Jesus!

47. Living in reverent fear of God means to live always aware that God is God, that there

4. Love, which is the unselfish caring for others; and

5. Long for spiritual nourishment so that they might grow.[48]

Such believers are people well-equipped to "proclaim God's mighty acts."

Peter tells the Christians that they are to rid themselves of all malice and pretense, envy and hurtful talk. Like babies at their mothers' breasts, these Christians are to drink the milk of God's kindness so that they might grow to maturity and wholeness, having received a foretaste of God's full mercy. Peter urges them to be like "living stones...built into a spiritual house," of strength that rests upon Jesus Christ, the cornerstone and foundation of this house. Peter writes, "Therefore prepare your minds for action; discipline yourselves; set all your hope on the grace that Jesus Christ will bring you . . . love one another deeply from the heart" (1:13, 22).

Later in the letter Peter writes, "Like good stewards of the manifold grace of God, serve one another with whatever gift each of you has received . . . whoever serves must do so with the strength that God supplies . . . ." (4:10–11).

In much of his letter, Peter paints a picture of a people, God's people, who can do the work of the kingdom, who can "proclaim God's mighty acts." Christians are to be unified and disciplined. We are to love one another. We are to serve one another. Peter reminds us that we are to be agreeable, sympathetic, and humble. We are not to retaliate when wronged. And we are to remember that we are part of something big!

Something Big

Read through any company's annual reports over the years and you'll find a common theme. Every year is "momentous" and "without precedent." Every year, according to the reports, management is faced with difficulties and challenges that have never been seen before. Listen to politicians and pundits. Even theologians and teachers. It seems that we always want to believe that we live in momentous times, perhaps the most important period in our nation's, or company's, or church's history. Why? Why is it

---

is an aspect of God's holiness that lies beyond rationality and morality. Rudolph Otto coined the word numinous to describe it. It is the "awesome-filled" overpowering-ness of God. It is energy. It is urgency. It is thunder, fire, and the "sound of sheer silence." It is why God can never be our "buddy."

48. *The New Oxford Annotated Bible with the Apocrypha, Third ed.*, Michael D. Cooper, Marc Z. Brettler, Carol A. Newsom, and Pheme Perkins, eds. (New York, NY: Oxford University Press, 2001), New Testament, p.396.

so important for us to believe we face challenges greater than anyone has faced before us?

It is because we all want to be part of something big. We want to be part of something that transcends the ordinariness of our daily lives. We need to believe that our lives and our work really matter. Thus, it is all the more odd that many Christians so easily marginalize "church." Church becomes a place to see friends for a while on Sunday morning, or a place where we come to learn a little more about how to be nice or how to be happy, or a place to which we turn in tough times—but certainly nothing BIG.

But in today's passage, Peter blows out of the water all attempts to marginalize church and faith. Christians, he writes, are a community chosen and formed by God so that we might proclaim God to the world, so that all those who are blind to God's "mighty acts" might see the truth.

Re-read verses 9 and 10. If Peter's words don't make your heart race at least a bit, then perhaps you have yet to experience the passion and even the sense of purpose that ought to mark believers. My church has talked a good bit about being passionate disciples so that we might be a passionate church. Why? So that we may effectively proclaim God to the world in what we say and in what we do— in who we are.

We are living through tough times, albeit much more so for some than for others, but all of us feel pressures and anxieties. Peter writes to encourage Christians who are being persecuted and shunned. He seeks to strengthen their resolve by reminding them of their true identities. They are the people of God, God's colonists as it were, who will never be abandoned by God and whose purpose can never be diminished. We are no less the people of God, chosen for a purpose larger than ourselves.

God has bestowed a great mercy on us, calling us to him and to his purposes. We must never pull back in the face of tough times, but always push forward. We must strive to hear God's voice and let him lead us with renewed purpose. Like those believers long ago, we can hear Peter calling us to be a people of deep faith pursuing a holy purpose with love, joy, discipline, humility, and courage so that we may extend to others the mercy that God has extended to us.

For a Deeper Understanding

A living stone . . . like living stones

In 1 Peter 2, Peter piles image upon image, metaphor upon metaphor. Peter begins by comparing the Christians to newborn infants who need "pure, spiritual milk" to grow up. What is that milk? Jesus, of course.

Then, Peter urges the Christians to come to Jesus, a "living stone." This stone has been evaluated by the world and found wanting, rejected and tossed aside. But, in truth, this living stone is precious beyond measure, chosen by God for God's purposes. Too much of the world is simply wrong about Jesus.

And as Jesus is the living stone, so are Christians "like living stones." We participate in the life of Christ. We are called to the imitation of Christ. Earlier in the letter, Peter quotes from Leviticus: "You shall be holy, for I am holy" (1:16). We, like living stones, are being built into a house, a "spiritual house," of which Jesus is the cornerstone (2:5-6). Those who reject the cornerstone stumble and fall, but those who respond in obedient faith are "a chosen people, a royal priesthood" (2:9 NIV).

In his commentary on 1 Peter, David Bartlett writes:

> . . . the difference between Christians and non-Christians is not that we see different things, but that we see the same things differently. Those who believe and those who do not both see Jesus Christ, the rock. For believers, that rock is the cornerstone or the capstone of their lives as individuals and in community. For unbelievers, that rock is simply to be rejected. What makes the difference between the two ways of seeing is faith. [49]

God's Chosen People?

Few topics are as perennially confusing to Christians as what we mean by "God's chosen people." And it can be emotionally charged, especially in light of some Christians' treatment of Jews over the centuries. But the best place to begin is seeking to understand what the biblical writers meant, particularly two Jews, Peter and Paul.

When God chose Abraham, God set about to form a people who would be his people. God would teach them what it meant to be his people. They would be a holy people, set apart for God's work. They would love God and love one another. Abraham's family would become the nation of Israel and, later, the people known as the Jews.

But what changed with the arrival of Jesus? Most Jews rejected Jesus as their Messiah and the movement, the Church, became overwhelmingly Gentile. So much so that Judaism and Christianity became like two rivers flowing away from one another.

But Paul and Peter are both Jews. Indeed, Paul is a Pharisee. Has Jesus given birth to a new "chosen people?" Are their fellow Jews who reject Jesus

---

49.   David L. Bartlett, "1st Peter" in *NIB*, vol. 12 (Nashville, TN: Abingdon, 1998), p.268.

still "God's chosen," still the elect of God? What does Peter mean when he calls the community of believers, "a chosen race, a royal priesthood, a holy nation, God's own people"?

In his letter to the Christians in Rome, Paul has to deal with these questions as he strives to unify the Jewish-Christians and the Gentile-Christians. What constitutes the people of God? A shared ethnicity? A common faith in God? How are the formerly pagan Gentile-Christians to see the failure of the Jews to keep the covenant they had made with God? Can the Jewish-Christians expect that the Gentile-Christians will keep the Jewish food laws, the Sabbath, the rite of circumcision, and so on?

For Paul, and in the end for Peter as well, this Jesus movement is not about "Jews converting to Christianity." Paul could never have thought in those terms. Paul doesn't see himself as having a new religion, but a reconfigured one – reconfigured around Jesus Christ. Though Paul is missionary to the Gentiles, his hope is that his fellow Jews will yet come into the family of Christ, that the broken off branches will be rejoined to the tree. Paul's heart is broken over the fact that so many of his fellow Jews have rejected Jesus, thereby removing themselves from God's people, at least for a while. But, at the same time, Paul believes that God will figure out a way to get them back in.

In the midst of God's work among the Gentiles and the unbelieving Jews, Paul writes, the Gentile Christians must not see Israel's "stumbling" as reason for any feelings of superiority. The Gentiles' salvation is bound up with Israel's. There is not one covenant (the new) which replaces another (the old) and there are not two covenants running alongside each other. There is one God, one Lord, one Spirit, one baptism—one covenant for Jew and Gentile alike.

For Paul, with the coming of Christ, there is one and only one badge of membership in the people of God: faith in Jesus Christ. This is the badge that identifies God's "chosen people." This and none other.

Chapter 18

The Sword of Truth

Revelation 1:9–16

I, John, your brother who share with you in Jesus the persecution and the kingdom and the patient endurance, was on the island called Patmos because of the word of God and the testimony of Jesus. I was in the spirit on the Lord's day, and I heard behind me a loud voice like a trumpet saying, "Write in a book what you see and send it to the seven churches, to Ephesus, to Smyrna, to Pergamum, to Thyatira, to Sardis, to Philadelphia, and to Laodicea." Then I turned to see whose voice it was that spoke to me, and on turning I saw seven golden lampstands, and in the midst of the lampstands I saw one like the Son of Man, clothed with a long robe and with a golden sash across his chest. His head and his hair were white as white wool, white as snow; his eyes were like a flame of fire, his feet were like burnished bronze, refined as in a furnace, and his voice was like the sound of many waters. In his right hand he held seven stars, and from his mouth came a sharp, two-edged sword, and his face was like the sun shining with full force.

Revelation 2:1–7 (MSG)

Write this to Ephesus, to the Angel of the church. The One with Seven Stars in his right-fist grip, striding through the golden seven-lights' circle, speaks: "I see what you've done, your hard, hard work, your refusal to quit. I know you can't stomach evil, that you weed out apostolic pretenders. I know your persistence, your courage in my cause, that you never wear out. But you walked away from your first love—why? What's going on with you, anyway? Do you have any idea how far you've fallen? A Lucifer fall! Turn back! Recover your dear early love. No time to waste, for I'm well on my way to removing your light from the golden circle. You do have this to your credit: You hate the Nicolaitan business. I hate it, too. Are your ears awake? Listen. Listen to the Wind Words, the Spirit blowing through the churches. I'm about to call each conqueror to dinner. I'm spreading a banquet of Tree-of-Life fruit, a supper plucked from God's orchard."

A Vision of Christ

What would it be like to see a vision of Jesus Christ? John sees a dramatically awe-inspiring Jesus who bears messages to seven Christian communities. It seems that the Ephesians are doing good work, but have lost their first love. Have we lost ours?

For most of my life, Revelation was this mysterious book at the back of my Bible. Once in a while, my interest would be aroused by some of the endless fascination with the end times that floats around the fringes of the church. Back in the 70's, I read Hal Lindsey's *The Late Great Planet Earth* in its first edition, which was fun but seemed far-fetched. I even took a class on Revelation from the Moody Bible Institute. I can't say I remember anything from it. In all, Revelation was about as disconnected from my Christian faith as my copy of *Business Week*. I can't say Revelation was frightening; it was just weird and easily set aside.

Ignoring Revelation all those years was my loss. I wish I could get the years back. Over the past ten years, I've come to see the power and the beauty of Revelation, and even more importantly, the message of hope and encouragement in its pages. Scholars such as Bruce Metzger, Christopher Rowland, David Aune, Craig Hill, and Craig Koester[50] have opened up the book for me.

The Helicopter View

Revelation is easier to understand if we grasp the big picture, what a professor of mine liked calling the "helicopter view." Broadly speaking, the book has three sections:

- Chapters 1-3 consist of John's opening vision of Christ, and Jesus' letters to seven churches in western Asia Minor.

- Chapters 4-11 focus on God, Christ, and a world that chooses to trust itself rather than its creator. In chapter 11, the unbelieving come to faith and the heavens ring out with the worship of God. In some ways, the book could end right there, but John's visions retell this story beginning in chapter 12.

---

50. If someone asks me for a book on Revelation, I urge them to pick up a copy of Craig R. Koester's *Revelation and the End of All Things* (Grand Rapids, MI: Eerdmans, 2001). More than any other, this book has helped me to grasp the narrative of Revelation and understand better the symbolism. It is very suitable for laypeople and received excellent reviews from biblical scholars.

- Chapters 12-22 are not a continuation of the story, but a second telling of the cosmic conflict between the creator and his idolatrous creation. This time the story focuses on Satan and a world in thrall to the powers that oppose God. This story culminates in God's victory through Jesus Christ, the judgment of all people, and the arrival of the long-awaited new heavens and earth. This is the completed restoration of the cosmos and of humanity's relationship with God.

The book of Revelation begins by telling us that it is just that: a revelation of Jesus Christ, given to him by God, that Jesus is to share with his servants. A revelation is simply an unveiling, a pulling back of the curtains so that we can see the truth about the world, about God, and about what is to come. We're told that these visions are prophetic and that we are to hear and keep them, implying that these are words we are to understand. How can we "keep what is written" if what is written makes no sense? Thus, the book itself often interprets for us the meaning of the most important symbolism.

John has been banished to the island of Patmos, where he has visions.[51] These begin with his opening vision of Christ. What he sees transcends the power of words to express directly, thus, much like the prophet Ezekiel, his descriptions center on comparisons; i.e., Jesus' voice is "like the sound of many waters." The vision draws heavily on the Son of Man imagery of Daniel 7, in which God, the Ancient One, gives the Son of Man dominion over creation. Jesus stands amid seven golden lampstands which, we are told by the book itself, represent seven churches. He holds seven stars in his hand, which we are again told in the book, represent the angels of each of the seven churches.

And the sword in Jesus' mouth? It's an image that we find only in Revelation, where the metaphor occurs four times, culminating in Jesus' victory on the battlefield (Revelation 19). The sword is probably a metaphor for the tongue, with its sharpness conveying the power of Christ's words. What Jesus speaks is the truth.[52] And he is about to tell it to the churches.

---

51. Though the early church held that this John was also the writer of the gospel and the New Testament letters bearing the name of John, this is almost certainly another John. Based on clues in the book, this John was probably Jewish and a native of Palestine who emigrated to Asia Minor. David Aune, in *Word Biblical Commentary*, vol. 52A, Revelation 1-5 (Grand Rapids, MI: Zondervan, 2014), speculates that John's knowledge of the seven Christian communities shows he was an itinerant Christian prophet in western Asia Minor. Most scholars hold that the book was written late in the first century, toward the end of the Roman emperor Domitian's reign (81–96AD).

52. Though commentators do not seem to make much of it, every time I come to this passage, I think of Hebrews 4:12–13: "Indeed, the word of God is living and active, sharper

The Letter to Ephesus

Ephesus was a large and important city on the western coast of Asia Minor (modern-day Turkey). The Ephesian Christians work hard for the kingdom, seeking to stay true to the authentic gospel. And they endure the persecutions and suffering thrown at them. They even hate the works of the Nicolaitans.[53] But, Jesus takes them to task nonetheless, for they have forgotten their "first love." In their diligent work for the church, these Christians were losing sight of what it was all about, their own love of Jesus Christ.

The truth of this letter speaks to us. How easy it is to let all our "doing" run away with us. It can certainly happen in our church work and it can happen in a marriage. A couple can get so busy with children, job, home, and the rest, that they wake up one day and realize that they've lost their love for each other. Where are they then? It is the love of the spouses, one for another, that is to be the foundation of their marriage. So it is that our love of Jesus is to be the foundation of our life in the church. It is necessary to our discipleship. Doing the work, without the love, leaves us as only an empty shell and an ineffective witness to God's love. Hmmm, hardly what you might expect from that "weird" book called Revelation.

For a Deeper Understanding

Apocalyptic Literature

In Greek, the word apocalypse means "unveiling" and it is often used to describe an entire genre of writing that was very popular in the 200 years before and the 200 years after Jesus. Authors used apocalyptic writing to describe momentous and cosmic events, often having to do with the end of the world. Apocalyptic writing was stuffed full of symbols and filled with all sorts of wild imagery. These writings report mysterious revelations and entail a cosmic transformation of the heavens and the earth, as well as a judgment of the dead. This literature seems very odd to us because we rarely read anything like it, but it was not odd in Jesus' day. In the Bible, the second half of the book of Daniel is another example of apocalyptic writing.

---

than any two-edged sword, piercing until it divides soul from spirit, joints from marrow; it is able to judge the thoughts and intentions of the heart. And before him no creature is hidden, but all are naked and laid bare to the eyes of the one to whom we must render an account." To my mind, this is another of those echoes of Scripture that God hopes we'll hear.

53.   We have no idea who these people were or what they taught. Mention of them in the letters to Ephesus and Smyrna are the only references in ancient literature. Whoever they were, it is clear that they opposed the gospel of Christ.

Like all apocalyptic writings, the book of Revelation is filled with many sorts of symbols. There are colors, numbers, animals, lamp stands, buildings, plants, and so on. Some are very easy to understand, some are more obscure, and the meanings of some are probably lost to us forever. It is important to realize that the symbols in apocalyptic literature weren't meant to conceal, but to reveal and to invest the writings with their cosmic significance. For example, in chapter 17, John is shown the Whore of Babylon who drinks the blood of the saints. We might wonder who the Whore is, but the answer is provided in verse 9, where we are told that the woman is seated on seven mountains. Anyone in the ancient world would hear this as a very thinly veiled reference to the Seven Hills of Rome, for it was Rome who persecuted the Christians. Another prominent symbol is the number seven, which signifies completeness or totality. The seven heads of the dragon indicate Satan's total opposition to God (Rev 12:3); the seven spirits of the Lamb signify the fullness of the Holy Spirit going out with total power (seven horns) and full knowledge and insight (seven eyes). In the book of Revelation there are even seven beatitudes! All these symbols seem strange to us, but they were not strange to readers of ancient apocalyptic literature, in which seven always symbolized completeness.

As Christians, we believe that Jesus' death and resurrection was the most important event in human history, inaugurating God's new world—a world reborn. Easter was a thunderous moment—a moment when the ages met. Every Easter we celebrate God's victory over evil, sin, and death. We celebrate new creation and life beyond the grave!

Could any words really begin to describe such events? Because our everyday language would be woefully inadequate to the task, John uses enormously provocative and fantastical word-pictures to convey the enormity of these cosmic events. He writes to encourage persecuted Christians, to show them, as powerfully as he can, that the Christian story will end well, that their own story will end well, even though the abominations of Rome make this claim seem absurd. He reminds them of the cosmic powers they battle, a battle climaxing in Jesus' victory (Chapter 19 and 20) and inaugurating the final re-creation of "a new heaven and a new earth" (21:1) where "anyone who wishes [can] take the water of life as a gift" (22:17).

Chapter 19

The Lion and the Lamb

Revelation 5

Then I saw in the right hand of the one seated on the throne a scroll written on the inside and on the back, sealed with seven seals; and I saw a mighty angel proclaiming with a loud voice, "Who is worthy to open the scroll and break its seals?" And no one in heaven or on earth or under the earth was able to open the scroll or to look into it. And I began to weep bitterly because no one was found worthy to open the scroll or to look into it. Then one of the elders said to me, "Do not weep. See, the Lion of the tribe of Judah, the Root of David, has conquered, so that he can open the scroll and its seven seals." Then I saw between the throne and the four living creatures and among the elders a Lamb standing as if it had been slaughtered, having seven horns and seven eyes, which are the seven spirits of God sent out into all the earth. He went and took the scroll from the right hand of the one who was seated on the throne. When he had taken the scroll, the four living creatures and the twenty-four elders fell before the Lamb, each holding a harp and golden bowls full of incense, which are the prayers of the saints. They sing a new song: "You are worthy to take the scroll and to open its seals, for you were slaughtered and by your blood you ransomed for God saints from every tribe and language and people and nation; you have made them to be a kingdom and priests serving our God, and they will reign on earth. Then I looked, and I heard the voice of many angels surrounding the throne and the living creatures and the elders; they numbered myriads of myriads and thousands of thousands, singing with full voice, "Worthy is the Lamb that was slaughtered to receive power and wealth and wisdom and might and honor and glory and blessing!" Then I heard every creature in heaven and on earth and under the earth and in the sea, and all that is in them, singing, "To the one seated on the throne and to the Lamb be blessing and honor and glory and might forever and ever!" And the four living creatures said, "Amen!" And the elders fell down and worshiped.

The Throne Room of God

Who is it that we worship? How would you describe Jesus Christ and his relationship to God and to the cosmos—and to us?

A quick review of Revelation: John writes that he has been given the revelation of Jesus Christ, which is to be heard and kept. John's first vision is of an awe-inspiring Jesus, whose mouth is the sword of truth. Jesus has letters for seven churches, who represent the church universal. These are churches in western Asia Minor in the vicinity of Ephesus. Then, in chapter 4, John is whisked away to the heavens, to the very throne room of God. The image of the ancient one is like that of precious stones and he is surrounded by an emerald-like rainbow, as in Ezekiel 1:26–28.[54] Around the throne, John sees twenty-four other thrones on which are seated twenty-four elders. It is hard to be sure of the significance of twenty-four, though the simplest and probably best explanation is that the twenty-four elders represent the twelve tribes of Israel and the twelve apostles.

From the throne emanate power and might, as thunder rolls amidst lightning. In front of the throne are seven torches representing the seven archangels who stand before the throne of God (also 1:4, 3:1, 5:6, 8:2, and even Luke 1:19). Also in front of the throne is what John describes as a sea that is as calm as glass.

Around the throne are four living creatures. They have eyes in front and behind, signifying that they see everything and guard the throne. These creatures are cherubim (plural of cherub).[55] This image again draws on Ezekiel, this time 1:10, where there are four cherubim, though each has four faces. Here, the four faces (human, lion, ox, and eagle) are the same, but each cherub has only one face. All four cherubim have six wings (Isaiah 6:2). The four faces of the cherubim are meant to represent the entire created order, which becomes evident when their Amen awaits the joining in of all creation (5:13-14).[56]

Worship

And what are the creatures and the elders doing? They are worshiping. The cherubim sing praises to God's holiness – without ceasing, as if they

---

54. Revelation is dependent on the Old Testament, and I include a few references. It is natural that John would follow the prophets' descriptions of their visions as he attempts to put his own experiences into words.

55. This is pretty far removed from the way that we've come to think of cherubs, the fat little winged angels often equipped with a bow and arrow.

56. David Aune's three-volume commentary on Revelation in the *Word Biblical Commentary* is a big help in sorting through the symbolism. He also wrote the Revelation study notes in *The HarperCollins Study Bible*. A competent guide to the symbols can take away much of the mystery, just as people 2,000 years from now will need a guide to sort through the symbolism from our own time. For example, who in the future will associate a cherry tree with truth-telling?

had been created for this sole purpose. The elders fall on the ground in their worship, casting their crowns before the throne. Before this scene closes, all of creation joins in the worship of the Creator.

Often, when we come to Revelation, we are anxious to race on to the mysterious and scary scenes of beasts and destruction and special numbers. But the book is built around several dramatic and lengthy scenes of worship. They are the book's center. Indeed, chapters 4 and 5 are the heart of the Revelation given to John, not the endlessly fascinating four horsemen of the apocalypse.

The Lion and The Lamb

Yet, amidst this worship there is soon mourning and tears. The one on the throne holds a scroll that, unlike most papyri, is written on front and back. It is sealed with seven seals, which signifies that the seal is completely and utterly closed, for seven is the number of completion and totality. What does the scroll contain? We are not told. It could be God's plan for creation, or it could be the rest of the book. Whatever the scroll contains, there is no one, in all the heavens and the earth, who is worthy to open it and John weeps because the scroll will remain closed. Or might there be someone who is worthy?

One of the twenty-four elders comes to John and tells him that the Lion of Judah is worthy to open the scroll. Thus, we'd expect that John would turn to see a lion, the symbol of power and strength, standing ready to open the scroll.

Yet, when John turns, he doesn't see a lion at all. He sees a lamb. But not a cute, white, leaping little lamb. John sees a Lamb standing there as if it had been slaughtered! This is such a powerful moment in Revelation. John hears "Lion" but sees "Lamb." The contrast couldn't be more striking. We think we know what power and might are, but Jesus Christ has revealed that the truth is far from our expectation. It is the Lamb who conquers. Craig Koester writes:

> What John hears about the Lion recalls promises from the Old Testament, and what he sees in the lamb reflects the crucifixion of Christ. Both images point to the same reality. According to the Old Testament, God promised to send a powerful and righteous ruler. These promises are not rejected but fulfilled through the slaughtered yet living Lamb, who is not a hapless victim but a figure of royal strength.[57]

---

57. Craig R. Koester, *Revelation and the End of All Things* (Grand Rapids, MI: Eerdmans, 2001), p. 78.

And strong the Lamb certainly is. The Lamb has seven eyes, all-seeing and all-present (see Zechariah 4:10), and seven horns, all-powerful, as horns were ancient symbols of kingly power. In Revelation there are twenty-eight references to the exalted Lamb. It is the victorious Lamb of God from the end of the book who is often shown in stained glass windows.

The Lamb then takes the scroll from the hand of God, causing all the elders and cherubim to fall down before the Lamb in worship, singing their acknowledgement that the Lamb, and the Lamb alone, is worthy to open the scroll.

Then angels too numerous to count join the elders and the cherubim in their worship of the Lamb. The crescendo presses forward as all the creatures of all the cosmos join in the praise of the one seated on the throne and of the Lamb. Finally, the four living creatures say "Amen!"

How cold a heart it would be that could be unmoved by this scene! Imagine for a moment that you are a Christian who is being persecuted. What would these words say to you? Who is really in control of this world? To whom should every knee bow and tongue confess?

Would this not encourage you to persevere and to trust that God and the Lamb will be victorious over the powers that persecute you, even if it doesn't always seem that way? It is as if the curtains of heaven have been pulled back, revealing to you the truth of what is and who is. We shouldn't be surprised that it is this scene around which Handel composed the glorious final chorus in his Messiah.

For a Deeper Understanding

Symbolism

The Jews were not a sea-faring people. In their apocalyptic writings, the sea was always a symbol of chaos and terror, the birthplace of monsters (see Daniel 7). But, here, around the throne of God, the sea is calm—there is no chaos.

The "Lamb standing as if it had been slaughtered" calls on two key Old Testament images. The first is the Passover lamb, whose blood was spread on the doorway of the Hebrews so that the death of the firstborn would pass them by (Exodus 12). Of course, Jesus' last meal with his disciples was a Passover meal reshaped around Jesus' body and blood, representing a New Exodus. But the image of the Lamb here also evokes Isaiah 53, the story of the suffering servant who would take upon himself the iniquities of us all. A Christian could scarcely read Isaiah 53 and not see in it the story of Jesus' sacrifice.

By the end of the second century, Christians were using the four faces of the cherubim in their writing and art to symbolize the writers of the four gospels. The human face symbolized Matthew because he begins his gospel with a genealogy. Mark was the lion because his opening reference to Jesus as "Son of God" speaks of power and strength. Luke was the ox because he begins his gospel in the temple, where oxen were sometimes sacrificed. John was the eagle because his opening with Jesus as "the Word" points to Jesus' heavenly origins. In the ancient understanding of the cosmos, the heavens were "up there."[58]

---

58.   Koester, p.73.

PART IV
TO TAKE ACTION

We live in a time when it seems as if the world is awash in love, even though there is so much bitter division. How could this be? Sadly, for too many, love has devolved into a mere sentiment. But as Jesus said, anyone can love those who love them; it is loving the rest of the world that is the problem. In the Bible, love is never simply a feeling; love is something you do. It is sharing a kindness or a meal, caring for strangers, choosing not to return slights in kind. Love is a verb. How do we know God loves us? Look at the cross, Paul would say. It is all you need to know. Thus, there are significant portions of the New Testament where the word love does not appear. How odd that must seem to a world that thinks it knows what love is. Indeed, it probably strikes us all as odd that love is never used, as either a noun or verb in the Acts of the Apostles. But, of course, love is all over the book of Acts, for it is seen in countless actions. Love is what you do, not what you feel.

Do Justice

Micah 6:8 (NIV)
He has shown you, O mortal, what is good. And what does the LORD require of you?
To act justly and to love mercy and to walk humbly with your God.

Jeremiah 7:1–7, 11 (NIV)
This is the word that came to Jeremiah from the LORD: "Stand at the gate of the LORD's house and there proclaim this message: 'Hear the word of the LORD, all you people of Judah who come through these gates to worship the LORD. This is what the LORD Almighty, the God of Israel, says: Reform your ways and your actions, and I will let you live in this place. Do not trust in deceptive words and say, "This is the temple of the LORD, the temple of the LORD, the temple of the LORD!" If you really change your ways and your actions and deal with each other justly, if you do not oppress the foreigner, the fatherless or the widow and do not shed innocent blood in this place, and if you do not follow other gods to your own harm, then I will let you live in this place, in the land I gave your ancestors for ever and ever. . . . Has this house, which bears my Name, become a den of robbers to you? But I have been watching!' declares the Lord.

Mark 11:15–17 (NIV)
On reaching Jerusalem, Jesus entered the temple courts and began driving out those who were buying and selling there. He overturned the tables of the money changers and the benches of those selling doves, and would not allow anyone to carry merchandise through the temple courts. And as he taught them, he said, "Is it not written: 'My house will be called a house of prayer for all nations'? But you have made it 'a den of robbers.'"

It seems so straight-forward: Do justice. But do we? What does God require of us? Simply this: that we would do justice, love mercy, and walk humbly with God (Micah 6:8). These three simple phrases give shape to the sort of life God would have us lead and the choices God would have us make. Though the three phrases make a unified whole, each of them is built on a very important biblical word. Let's consider the first of them, justice (*mispat* in the Hebrew). Here's a sampling of some notable Old Testament passages on justice:

Hosea 12:6 (NIV)
But you must return to your God; maintain love and justice, and wait for your God always.

Amos 5:21-24 (NIV)
I hate, I despise your religious festivals; your assemblies are a stench to me. Even though you bring me burnt offerings and grain offerings, I will not accept them. Though you bring choice fellowship offerings, I will have no regard for them. Away with the noise of your songs! I will not listen to the music of your harps. But let justice roll on like a river, righteousness like a never-failing stream.

Isaiah 1:16-17 (NIV)
Wash and make yourselves clean. Take your evil deeds out of my sight; stop doing wrong. Learn to do right; seek justice. Defend the oppressed. Take up the cause of the fatherless; plead the case of the widow.

Jeremiah 9:24 (NIV)
"but let the one who boasts boast about this: that they have the understanding to know me, that I am the LORD, who exercises kindness, justice and righteousness on earth, for in these I delight," declares the LORD.

Justice

I don't think we often speak of "doing" justice, but the simple verb "do" captures the biblical meaning perfectly. In Scripture, justice is something we do. It is an action. It is never merely taking note of inequities or wrong. Justice is doing something about them. When we see a person being wronged by another, it is never enough simply to note the wrong, sigh in sympathy, and move on. "Doing justice" is correcting that wrong. Further, across the biblical story, justice is specifically about looking after the interests of those who cannot look after their own: the poor, the immigrant, the widow, and orphan. The biblical view is that the rich and powerful can do a pretty fine job looking after themselves; the poor cannot.

The importance to God of our doing justice is seen in the dramatic stories of two men: the prophet Jeremiah and the Christ, Jesus.

Jeremiah

About six centuries before Jesus, the prophet Jeremiah makes his way to the Temple gate. There, he stands in front of the massive doors and confronts his fellow Israelites. God's people have driven themselves over a cliff and now there is no turning back. It is too late; it is a "done deal" (see Jeremiah 4:28 for example). They have passed the point of no return. The "ifs" of Jeremiah 7:5–7 are not about righting the ship or drawing back from the brink, as was the case in other times. Instead, Jeremiah drives home the point that the time of reckoning has come. The "ifs," the warnings, proved fruitless before and now the poison fruit that the people have grown is about to be their undoing. They have not done justice and now they would reap the consequences. A few decades after Jeremiah's pronouncement, the Babylonian Empire rolls over Jerusalem, exiles tens of thousands of Jews, and destroys the majestic temple built by Solomon.

Why did this happen? Certainly, the biblical view is that it was God's judgment, a verdict rendered and carried out. A fair verdict, a just verdict. The people grasp that it is their own sin that is their undoing; yes, they have abandoned God and, yes, they have failed to do justice.

Jesus

If we go forward six centuries from Jeremiah, we again find a prophet charging into the Temple pronouncing God's judgment. But this time the prophet's name is Jesus. And as with Jeremiah, a few decades after Jesus' pronouncement, the Roman Empire rolls over Jerusalem, kills hundreds of thousands of Jews, and destroys the majestic temple built by Herod the Great. Seventy years after that, the Romans finish the job, clearing the Jews out of the area and erasing the Roman province of Judea from their geography books.

Many people don't grasp what it really means when Jesus invokes the words and actions of Jeremiah at the temple in Jerusalem. They forget that when the disciples are gawking at the magnificence of the temple, Jesus tells them that the giant stones were going to be thrown down (Mark 13:1–2; Matthew 24:1–3; Luke 21:5–7). If you visit Jerusalem today, you can see the giant cut stones that were levered off the temple mount by the Romans in 70 AD. They still sit on the sidewalks below, right where they fell.

For many people, the Babylonian exile and the destruction of Jerusalem by the Romans conjures up images of a God who looks for every transgression, great and small, and then smites the offender—judge, jury, and warden all rolled into one. But what does the Bible really say about judgment and punishment? Is it truly God's retribution, i.e. a smiting?

In a word, no. There is, instead, a moral causality in God's creation, a moral fabric in which actions have consequences, just as they do in the physical world. Sadly, sin is quite real and leads to often horrifying consequences. We see this in our lives all too often. Sometimes we say, "what goes around, comes around" or we allude to the parable when we say, "we reap what we sow." Abuse others and you'll find yourself abused. Treat others with kindness and you'll find that it too boomerangs back to you. These commonplace observations about life get us close to what the Bible teaches about God's judgment and the "punishment" that ensues.

We, of course, ask where God is as we suffer the consequences of our wrongful actions, as we plunge over the cliff. We sometimes make the mistake of thinking that God promises to insulate us from all the troubles of life, those of our making and those that are not. But this is not God's promise. However, God does promise us restoration after the fall. God does promise that he will never abandon us.

It isn't that God is always waiting to catch us when we fall; it is truer to say that God is always ready to restore us after the fall. The choices we and others make every day are often destructive and carry terrible consequences. Sometimes those choices are seen in the actions we take; in others, they are seen in our inaction and the blind eye we turn to those we could help. Just as Jeremiah forthrightly tells the people of the destruction and exile that lie ahead, he also brings them messages of hope and restoration. Yes, they are going over the cliff and the crash at the bottom will be terrifying, but God will still be with them and will bring them new life and new hope even in exile. (See Jeremiah 30 for some of these promises.)

And so we are called to "let justice roll on like a river, righteousness like a never-failing stream! (Amos 5:24 NIV).

For a Deeper Understanding

Den of Robbers = Cave of Brigands?

In his commentary *Mark for Everyone*, N.T. Wright helps us to understand what Jeremiah and Jesus meant by calling the temple a "den of robbers" (NIV).

. . . Although God had promised to bless Israel through the Temple, if Israel began to take it for granted . . . then the Temple itself could and would be judged. That's what the early chapters of Jeremiah are all about, including the quotation that comes here: God's house has become a brigand's cave.

In what sense was it a brigand's cave? Not in the sense that people were using it to make money on the side. The word 'brigand', in Jesus' day, wasn't a word for 'thief' or 'robber' in the ordinary sense, but for the revolutionaries, those we today would call the ultra-orthodox, plotting and ready to use violence to bring about their nationalist dreams.

Part of Jesus' charge against his fellow Jews was that Israel as a whole had used its vocation, to be the light of the world, as an excuse for a hard, narrow, nationalist piety and politics in which the rest of the world was to be, not enlightened, but condemned.... Violence towards outsiders; injustice towards Israel itself; that was what the Temple had come to mean. As with the fig tree, Jesus' only word for the place was one of judgment.

How did his actions in the Temple mean that? . . . The sacrificial system, and with it the reason for the Temple's existence, depended on money-changing and animal purchase. By stopping the entire process, even just for a short but deeply symbolic moment, Jesus was saying, more powerfully than any words could express: the Temple is under God's judgment. Its reason for existing is being taken away.[59]

There is a passage in Ezekiel that helps us grasp Wright's main point. The temple priests, especially the High Priest, were the leaders of Israel, but they had been poor shepherds (Ezekiel 34:1-11), leading the people away from God rather than toward God. It was an old, tragic story, for God's people had been so poorly led for so very long. And now, in Jesus, God's judgment is falling on the temple and all its many corrupt systems, just as God's judgment had fallen on the temple six centuries before in the form of the Babylonians. God simply cannot abide injustice, and those who lead have a higher responsibility to get it right . . . as do those who teach (James 3:1).

---

59. N. T. Wright, *Mark for Everyone*, New Testament for Everyone series, (Louisville, KY: Westminster John Knox Press, 2004).

Chapter 21

More Than a Many-Splendored Thing

1 Corinthians 13:4-7, 11-13
Love is patient; love is kind; love is not envious or boastful or arrogant or rude. It does not insist on its own way; it is not irritable or resentful; it does not rejoice in wrongdoing, but rejoices in the truth. It bears all things, believes all things, hopes all things, endures all things. . . . When I was a child, I spoke like a child, I thought like a child, I reasoned like a child; when I became an adult, I put an end to childish ways. For now we see in a mirror, dimly, but then we will see face to face. Now I know only in part; then I will know fully, even as I have been fully known. And now faith, hope, and love abide, these three; and the greatest of these is love.

1 John 3:16–17, 4:7–11
We know love by this, that he laid down his life for us—and we ought to lay down our lives for one another. How does God's love abide in anyone who has the world's goods and sees a brother or sister in need and yet refuses help? Beloved, let us love one another, because love is from God; everyone who loves is born of God and knows God. Whoever does not love does not know God, for God is love. God's love was revealed among us in this way: God sent his only Son into the world so that we might live through him. In this is love, not that we loved God but that he loved us and sent his Son to be the atoning sacrifice for our sins. Beloved, since God loved us so much, we also ought to love one another.

Love Is . . .

Love is . . . what? That is the question. If we are going to get anywhere close to understanding, we have to begin with the biblical meaning of love. And this will not be easy for us. The gulf between the biblical and the secular understandings of love is so vast that it renders the word love nearly useless to us. For much of the world, love is all about romance and wonderful feelings. It is about that ecstatic experience of new love, of being "in love" which, as exhilarating as it might be, is no more than the light of a candle compared to the brilliant sunlight that is God's love, a love to which God calls us. So, we'll try to come to this topic with a bit of a blank slate. There are three keys to the biblical understanding of love:

> Love is a bond of total trust and commitment;
> Love is about actions, not feelings; and
> The best synonym for love is sacrifice.

Trust and Commitment

Though there are many dimensions of love in the Old Testament, including the romantic and sexual in the Song of Solomon, the dominant love theme is one of covenant. God loves his people and the people are to love God within the bounds of a covenant that binds them in mutual obligation. Though the covenant is never devoid of passion, it is focused upon trust, high regard for each other, faithfulness, and obedience. God uses marriage as a metaphor for this covenantal love. For example, the people are not to commit "adultery" against God by chasing after false gods. Seven centuries before Jesus, God would speak through his prophet Hosea of his love for his people in shockingly personal terms. There was simply no parallel in the ancient cultures.

Jesus and the New Testament writers build upon the Old Testament understanding of love. Indeed, Jesus clears up any possible confusion about this covenantal love. Love is total trust, total commitment.—the neighbor, whom we are to love, becomes anyone in need, even (especially?) our enemy. And, as in the Old Testament, this is no abstract love of humanity—it is about what we do. Authentic love calls us to the hard work of repentance and discipline, of forgiveness and caring.

Actions, Not Feelings

In keeping with the Old Testament law, Jesus teaches that the two greatest commandments are to love God and neighbor, though he actually doesn't throw around the word love very often. Instead, Jesus speaks of mercy, caring, kindness, and forgiveness. Jesus, and later Paul, constantly reminds the disciples that love is not about what we feel, it is about what we do. Are we patient with others? Are we kind? Do we resist the temptation to boast or envy? Do we avoid being irritable toward others? (1 Corinthians 13:4). Understanding that love is about actions, not sentiment, makes sense of Jesus' teaching to "love your enemies" (Matthew 5:44). Though we may not have loving feelings toward our enemies, we can still be merciful, caring, and forgiving. We cannot control how we feel, but we can control what we do—and God calls us to "do love."

Love as Sacrifice

John cuts to the heart of this sacrificial love in 1 John 3:16: "We know love by this, that he laid down his life for us—and we ought to lay down our lives for one another." What the New Testament means by love is the cross. The cross is the concrete embodiment of love. God so loved the world that he gave up the life of his own son. Jesus so loved us all that he laid down his own life. If we want to know what love is, look to the cross. The essence of love is sacrifice. Love is self-giving, never self-seeking.[60] What might this mean in the context of our relationships?

For a Deeper Understanding

Eros, Phileo, and Agape

If we really want to grasp the biblical perspective of love, we need to begin with the Greek word choices made by the New Testament writers.

Eros is a Greek word that has been taken directly into English. For the ancient Greeks, *eros* was the passionate love that desired the other for oneself. Often equated with sexual lust and fulfillment, the basic idea is that of erotic intoxication or ecstasy. *Eros* is never used by the New Testament writers. Paul could have used this word in his discussions of love and marriage, but he does not. This choice begins to point us in the biblical direction—love is never about the fulfillment of our own desires, regardless of how powerful or wonderful the experience might be.

Phileo (a verb) is a Greek word that is a little more familiar than you might think. After all, Philadelphia is the city of brotherly love. *Phileo* carries the sense of relatedness, specifically, to treat someone as if they are one of your own people. For example, we sometimes treat someone as if they are

---

60. Richard B. Hays, *The Moral Vision of the New Testament: Community, Cross, New Creation, A Contemporary Introduction to New Testament Ethics* (New York, NY: HarperSanFrancisco, 1996). For Hays, the three focal images of the New Testament are community, cross, and new creation. Love is best understood as an interpretation of the cross.

a member of our family —that would be *philia* (the noun form). The New Testament writers use *phileo* infrequently. There is little theological significance to its occasional use (only about twenty times). *Phileo* is often used synonymously with *agape*, the New Testament word for love.

Agape is used about 250 times by the New Testament writers. Just as significant, when Greek-speaking Jews translated the Hebrew Old Testament into Greek, they almost exclusively used *agape*. Why did they choose this word?

Agape was used very little by Greek writers in the ancient world. It is a weak word, lacking the power of *eros* and the warmth of *phileo*. Perhaps the best way to describe *agape* is "colorless." It just doesn't have a lot of meaning—which makes it perfect for the Biblical authors! No common Greek word really means what they wanted to say.

Because *agape* is a colorless word, its meaning to the original readers of the New Testament comes solely from its context. The biblical translators and authors know that the scriptural meaning of love, God's meaning, is far different from what the world means by love. If they use *eros* or *phileo*, readers will bring to Scripture many misconceptions. But by using *agape*, this infrequent Greek word, Paul, Matthew, John, and the rest could bring God's meaning to it.

We have in our minds certain meanings of the word love, whether it is romance or friendship or something else. We need to set all those aside and let Paul define love for us as he writes, "Love is patient . . . kind . . . not envious or boastful or arrogant . . . ."

Chapter 22

Loving from Our Center

Ecclesiastes 4:9–12
Two are better than one, because they have a good reward for their toil. For if they fall, one will lift up the other; but woe to one who is alone and falls and does not have another to help. Again, if two lie together, they keep warm; but how can one keep warm alone? And though one might prevail against another, two will withstand one. A threefold cord is not quickly broken.

Romans 12:9–18 (MSG)
Love from the center of who you are; don't fake it. Run for dear life from evil; hold on for dear life to good. Be good friends who love deeply; practice playing second fiddle. Don't burn out; keep yourselves fueled and aflame. Be alert servants of the Master, cheerfully expectant. Don't quit in hard times; pray all the harder. Help needy Christians; be inventive in hospitality. Bless your enemies; no cursing under your breath. Laugh with your happy friends when they're happy; share tears when they're down. Get along with each other; don't be stuck-up. Make friends with nobodies; don't be the great somebody. Don't hit back; discover beauty in everyone. If you've got it in you, get along with everybody.

Love from the Center

Do we love from the center? Are we a good friend who loves deeply? What questions should we be asking ourselves about our relationships?

As I write this, I am thinking about a dear friend, one of our ministers, whose memorial service was the next day. More than most people I have known, this friend loved from the center. She never faked it.

I never heard an unkind word from her about another person. No matter how much her illness was making her hurt, she always had a smile. She was "cheerfully expectant" in all things. No matter how hard things got for her, she never quit, never gave up. Indeed, she probably pushed herself too hard in her determination to go about the making of disciples of Jesus Christ despite her illness.

She taught me a lot about praying, especially when things got toughest. She was a good friend to so many. She never insisted on being the "great somebody." I doubt there was anyone that she didn't get along with. She loved from the center: her strong, kind, Spirit-filled, wise, loving center.

I'm sure I could have learned a lot more from my friend about relationships had I been a better and more willing student. But, for me, and many men, relationships are not always at the top of our list, no matter how much we profess that we love God and neighbor. In his book, *Chazown*, Craig Groeschel admits that "for years, I didn't see the value of intentionally developing godly relationships. That was my wife's department, so I left the relational ball in her court. Content with following along, I struggled relationally, not seeing the value of investing in and receiving from them."[61] Sounds a lot like me and other men I know. We know with our heads and even our hearts that we proclaim a relational God who desires love from us before all else—love for God and love of others. But when it comes to the real work of relationships, too many men back off, unsure of how to proceed and even unwilling to try.

What Love Looks Like

Opening with a telling "therefore," Romans 12 marks a turn in Paul's letter. But it is not the turn people often think is taken. Some contrast Paul's "theology" (Chapters 1–11) with his "ethics" (Chapters 12–16), perhaps describing it as "belief" and "practice." But this does Paul a disservice. There can be no such separation for Paul or for us. What we "believe" and what we "do" are woven together and cannot be pulled apart. Both the intellectually-minded and the ever-practical find it more comfortable to put belief and practice in two separate boxes. As N.T. Wright aptly notes, "They are the breath and blood of Christian living, the twin signs of life."[62]

Romans 1–11 takes us up a mountain, showing us that God's faithfulness to the covenant made with Abraham and the Israelites has been brought to its fulfillment in Jesus Christ. And with Jesus' arrival nothing

---

61. *Chazown* (pronounced khaw-zone) is Hebrew for dream, revelatation, or vision. Craig Groeschel, *Chazown Revised and Updated Edition: Discover and Pursue God's Purpose for Your Life* (Colorado Springs, CO: Multnomah, 2017), p.127.

62. N. T. Wright, *NIB*, vol. 10: *Acts, Romans, 1 Corinthians* (Nashville, TN: Abingdon, 2002), p.700.

can ever be the same. Creation and humanity have been remade, even as we await this re-creation's final consummation.

In Romans 12, Paul begins to show us, concretely, what this re-creation looks like. We are transformed by the renewing of our minds, so that we may see clearly what is "good and acceptable and perfect," so that we can imaginatively comprehend and embrace the will of God (12:2). This renewal does not take place in isolation, but in relationship within the community. Our reshaping plays out differently from person to person, but all of it is given to us for the building up of the community (12:3–8).

And what does this renewing of our minds look like? It looks like love. And what does love look like? Love is genuine, coming from the center of ourselves. It can't be faked. Love is sacrificial. It is mutual. It is being willing to play second fiddle. Love is taking care of those who need us or are simply in need. We laugh with our friends when they laugh and we cry with them when they mourn.

Read Romans 12:9–18 again. Read it with different translations. Try reading it less as a series of exhortations and more as a description, an imaginative description of the renewed mind living with others, including even those who are hostile to us or to the Gospel of Christ.

All understandings of love that exclude God are mere distortions of the real thing. Thus, Paul tells the Christians in Rome that they are to love but then has to tell them exactly what genuine God-given love looks like, so that they can despise what is evil and hold on to what is good (12:9).

All this takes more imagination than we think. The world wants to teach us about love, to have us conform to its ways. In the memorable words of scholar and biblical translator J.B. Phillips, "the world wants to squeeze us into its mold." So we must train ourselves to recognize the face of Christian love. Let that face be yours today.

Chapter 23

Love Matters

Mark 12:28–34, 38–44

One of the scribes came near and heard them disputing with one another, and seeing that he answered them well, he asked him, "Which commandment is the first of all?" Jesus answered, "The first is, 'Hear, O Israel: the Lord our God, the Lord is one; you shall love the Lord your God with all your heart, and with all your soul, and with all your mind, and with all your strength.' The second is this, 'You shall love your neighbor as yourself.' There is no other commandment greater than these." Then the scribe said to him, "You are right, Teacher; you have truly said that 'he is one, and besides him there is no other', and 'to love him with all the heart, and with all the understanding, and with all the strength,' and 'to love one's neighbor as oneself,'—this is much more important than all whole burnt offerings and sacrifices." When Jesus saw that he answered wisely, he said to him, "You are not far from the kingdom of God." After that no one dared to ask him any question.

As he taught, he said, "Beware of the scribes, who like to walk around in long robes, and to be greeted with respect in the marketplaces, and to have the best seats in the synagogues and places of honor at banquets! They devour widows' houses and for the sake of appearance say long prayers. They will receive the greater condemnation." He sat down opposite the treasury, and watched the crowd putting money into the treasury. Many rich people put in large sums. A poor widow came and put in two small copper coins, which are worth a penny. Then he called his disciples and said to them, "Truly I tell you, this poor widow has put in more than all those who are contributing to the treasury. For all of them have contributed out of their abundance; but she out of her poverty has put in everything she had, all she had to live on."

Contrasts

You want to know what love is? It is a matter of the heart. Meet this widow who gives from the heart, for that is all she has. She knows that love matters. The setting of the widow's penny story is important to appreciating this scripture passage. Jesus has entered Jerusalem to the waving of palm branches. He has wept over the city, knowing where things are headed. He has been to the temple, where, invoking the words and actions of Jeremiah, he has pronounced warnings against the temple, the nation, and all those who refuse to embrace Jesus and the path that he has laid before them. In response to all this, groups have come forward to trap Jesus in a mistake. The Pharisees have tried to trap him over the question of taxes. The Sadducees have tried to trap him over the question of the resurrection. Others have tried to use David's words against him. Now, a crowd is gathered around Jesus and his disciples as they sit in the temple courtyard. The stakes could not be higher.

Perhaps a little melodramatically, Jesus raises his voice so that everyone can hear him. He is ostensibly teaching his disciples but he wants to make sure that no one misses a thing! Jesus draws the crowd's attention to scribes walking through the temple. How they love to walk around so that all can see their importance. How they love the best seats, the places of honor, the deferential greetings—all as they consume the property of widows. One could hardly paint a more compelling picture of the worst in human pride and greed. And all this is directed at the scribes, those the crowd sees as the learned spiritual leaders of Israel! And it is in stark contrast to one scribe, who seemed to hear Jesus clearly and understand much about the nature of God's kingdom.

Jesus draws the crowd's attention to the chests in which visitors could place their temple offerings.[63] The rich were stopping by to drop in their gifts and Luke is clear that these are non-obligatory contributions. But Jesus points the listening crowd to a woman, a poor widow,[64] who drops two lepta in one of the chests. A lepta was the smallest value coin, equivalent to about 1/128th of the average daily wage! In a pointed comment, Jesus says that the rich gave out of their "left overs," [65] whereas the widow dropped into the chest all that she had. In contrast to the gifts of the rich, the widow has made hers out of a passionate and wholehearted commitment. For her, it was a matter of love pointedly expressed in how she used the little money she had.

63. Josephus, writer of a late first-century Jewish history, reports that there were thirteen collection chests located in the Court of the Women in the temple courtyards. Each chest was designated for a different use.

64. Widows were at the bottom of the social ladder and epitomized the needy. Under the Law of Moses, the Jews were obligated to look after the needs of widows and orphans.

65. John Nolland, *The Gospel of Matthew*, The New International Greek Testament Commentary (Grand Rapids, MI: Eerdmans, 2005).

A Growing Heart

Everyone grows into somebody. The only question is what sort of somebody. In the temple courtyard, Jesus draws a stark contrast. On the one hand, the scribes have allowed their many talents and their successes to grab hold of their hearts, turning them inward. They live for the trappings and privileges of the elite, perhaps blind to the harm they do. Indeed, at best, they have grown to be morally and spiritually blind; at worst, they have grown to be calculating exploiters of the weak.

We know nothing of the widow's life, but we do know that she has grown to have a heart that is passionately devoted to God's cause. She is destitute in a way that you and I can't imagine. There is no Social Security or Medicare. All she has is a couple of nearly worthless coins, yet she offers them to God. There is no reason to think she is a fool. She must know that her two lepta will make zero difference to the temple. But she knows that she gives not based upon what the temple needs, nor even what God needs, but out of her own need, her own faithful heart's need to give generously. It is her heart that matters, not her household budget. For her, it is a matter of love and Jesus knows that out of love, she has given far more than all the rich people lined up at the chests.

Love Matters

Is money really the point here? Of course not. Jesus is contrasting the hearts of the scribes and the rich with the heart of this lone widow. But Jesus also knows, as the crowd knows, that how people handle their money is a concrete expression of what they most value, where their hearts are. And there could be no more concrete demonstration of a committed, outwardly-focused heart than the widow dropping in the two nearly worthless coins. It is the concrete expression of her love for God, a love that encompasses her heart, mind, soul, and strength.

The scribes grow to be people focused inwardly, focused upon themselves. The rich give only token gifts, ensuring that their own social status will stay intact.[66] But the widow—despite her hardships—gives no concern to herself, but gives all she has for the benefit of others. This ought to remind us that none of us have been saved solely for our own benefit. We have been restored to a right relationship with God so that we may extend God's

---

66. In the Mediterranean cultures, the principal use for wealth was to acquire and maintain social status.

mercy and caring to others. We are to love God and love neighbor. Do we? How would someone know?

As believers striving to be evermore Christlike, we always have to remind ourselves of where our lives should be centered. That center is to be our Lord Jesus Christ, who is the incarnation of God's love. Nothing matters more.

For a Deeper Understanding

Who Were the Scribes?

There are various groups that swirl through and around the Gospel accounts, such as the Pharisees, Sadducees, priests, scribes, and more. Who were these groups? Specifically, in today's passage who were the scribes Jesus refers to?

In a general sense, a scribe was simply someone who could read and write. That doesn't seem like much of a distinction in our culture, but in the ancient world such people were pretty rare. In Jesus' day, perhaps less than ten to fifteen percent of the people were literate and many of those were barely so. Thus, we shouldn't be surprised that scribal classes developed in ancient cultures. Scribes came to be those who were able to gain the skills and education needed to build a career around their literacy.

Scribes were the educated intelligentsia and were widely respected for their learning. This would be especially true among the Jews who cherished the Word of God contained in the written Hebrew scrolls. For example, Ezra the scribe was sent by the Persian king to guide and instruct the inhabitants of Judea after the Babylonian exile. Ezra was an official in the Persian Empire and educated in the laws and customs of Israel (see Ezra 7).

The Jewish scribes in Jesus' day were leaders in the community and were often wealthy. They were easily susceptible to the twin temptations of pride and greed. Of course, who among us is immune to these temptations? There are many warnings to the early Christian leaders as well (Acts 4:32-5:11, 20:33-35; Romans 16:18; Philippians 3:19; 1 Peter 5:2–3; 2 Peter 2:3).

Chapter 24

A Good Steward

1 Peter 4:1–11

Since therefore Christ suffered in the flesh, arm yourselves also with the same intention (for whoever has suffered in the flesh has finished with sin), so as to live for the rest of your earthly life no longer by human desires but by the will of God. You have already spent enough time in doing what the Gentiles like to do, living in licentiousness, passions, drunkenness, revels, carousing, and lawless idolatry. They are surprised that you no longer join them in the same excesses of dissipation, and so they blaspheme. But they will have to give an accounting to him who stands ready to judge the living and the dead. For this is the reason the gospel was proclaimed even to the dead, so that, though they had been judged in the flesh as everyone is judged, they might live in the spirit as God does. The end of all things is near; therefore be serious and discipline yourselves for the sake of your prayers. Above all, maintain constant love for one another, for love covers a multitude of sins. Be hospitable to one another without complaining. Like good stewards of the manifold grace of God, serve one another with whatever gift each of you has received. Whoever speaks must do so as one speaking the very words of God; whoever serves must do so with the strength that God supplies, so that God may be glorified in all things through Jesus Christ. To him belong the glory and the power forever and ever. Amen.

We may live in a world with pain, loss, and hatred, but we have been born anew into a world of love, compassion, and forgiveness. Peter urges us to actually live this new life even as we strive to endure through tough times. God has given us many gifts, now as always. Our charge is to put them to good use to the glory of God.

A Tale of Two Worlds

As I've studied 1 Peter, I've been struck by how much sense this book makes as a letter written to encourage and comfort Christians who are going through very tough times. The suffering of the believers in Asia Minor is the ever-present subtext for the entire letter.

I'm also struck by how often Peter strikes the same themes in his letters as Paul. Mind you, these are two men who were sometimes at odds with one another as they, and all the early believers, worked through the implications of Jesus' death and resurrection. In his letters to the Galatians, Paul actually calls Peter out over the question of who will share a dining table with whom (Galatians 2:11-14; note, Paul calls Peter "Cephas," which is the Aramaic equivalent of the Greek "Petros/Peter," both meaning "rock.")

In today's passage, Peter, like Paul, contrasts two worlds, the world of the "flesh" (v. 6) and the world of the "spirit" (also, v. 6). The world of the flesh, as Peter puts it, is a world filled with "licentiousness, passions, drunkenness, revels, carousing, and lawless idolatry" (v. 3). In other words, this world of the flesh is a world driven by all that is wrong with us and all the wrong we do; in shorthand, it is a world of sin. In contrast, the world of the spirit is a world filled with constant love, hospitality, and good stewardship of the many gifts and graces God has given us (v. 8-10).

Now, you might think that all Peter has in mind is a call to Christian living, but that isn't all of it, not by half. Look at v. 7: "The end of all things is at hand." It is an echo of Jesus' first words in the Gospel of Mark: "The time is fulfilled, and the kingdom of God is at hand; repent, and believe in the good news" (Mark 1:15). Peter, like Paul, comes to understand that with Jesus' coming, this second world, the world of the spirit, the Kingdom of God, has arrived. And the believers have been given a new birth (1 Peter 1:3) into this world.

Yet, the fact that the "old" world, the world of the "flesh," is still around is as obvious to Peter and the believers as it is to you and me. They understand that Jesus' resurrection has changed everything; God's great plan to rescue humanity has already been accomplished, yet the project is not yet consummated. Somehow, they live in a period between the times, within both the age of the flesh and the age of the spirit.

The believers have been given a new birth into the age of the spirit; they are the ones "on whom the ends of the ages" has come (1 Corinthians 10:11). They are new creations who have been given "a new birth into a living hope through the resurrection of Jesus Christ from the dead, and into an inheritance that is imperishable, undefiled, and unfading, kept in heaven . . . " (1 Peter 1:3-4).

God's work in them is real, concrete, and undeniable. They could look back to their old lives even as they live their new life in Christ. Thus, Peter isn't merely urging them to live virtuously; Greek philosophers such as Epicurus did that all the time, as do thousands of self-help books of our own day. Peter is reminding them of who they are, urging them to live as the new people into whom God has already made them. It's akin to telling a teenager to act their age.

Living between the Times

If we have been given a new birth into a living hope, then what is the shape of this new birth, this new life in the Spirit? Both Peter and Paul have a great deal to say to believers as they help them to grasp the substance of this new life. Peter, here in v. 7-11, draws the Christians' attention to:

- Serious (clear-minded; thinking wisely) discipline for the sake of our prayers, by which Peter seems to mean that wisdom and discipline are the right soil for our prayers;

- "Above all" maintaining constant love for one another, for such love puts sin in our past, exactly where it belongs;

- Hospitality, which was an important norm across much of the ancient world;

- Being good stewards of the many gifts that God has given us;

- Taking care in our proclamation of God's Good News, for, looking back to 1 Peter 1:12, we speak of the things at which even the "angels long to look";

- Being ready to serve, for it is God who strengthens us in our work as we build God's kingdom.

As in Paul's letters, such lists for the new believers are not meant to be complete. Rather, they paint a picture of what living in the Spirit really looks like. Peter's brief words about gifts and stewardship are a good example.

Good Stewards

In one sentence (v. 10), Peter uses three key New Testament themes. First, we Christians have been given many gifts. Some we might refer to as our "talents," others we call our "possessions," and still others, we throw into the loose label, "spiritual gifts." But regardless of what we call them, they are all gifts from God. Our accomplishments and accumulations are not our own, but are entirely from God, for even life itself is God's gift to us.

Second, we are stewards of these gifts, not their owners. All our gifts, and they are just that, are given to us with purpose, God's purpose.

Third, we are given these gifts so we can serve. Whom are we called to serve? God and one another, or to clarify, God, through serving one another. Peter urges us, even in tough times, to look outside ourselves, to use what God has given us to strengthen the community that is God's people and to be a good witness to all those who have yet to be reborn. And all this is to God's glory!

For a Deeper Understanding

Paul on Gifts in the Church

Paul has a great deal to say in his letters about the gifts that God has given us. These gifts, of which Peter reminds us we are stewards, are both tangible and intangible, wide-ranging, and varied from person to person. Their purpose is to both build up the disciple of Christ and, more importantly, to build up the body of Christ. The following are some brief reflections on this from Richard Hays, a leading Pauline scholar.

> The church is a charismatic community. Paul is also insistent that the gifts of the Spirit must be exercised within the body of Christ for the benefit of the community as a whole. This leads him to highlight the twin themes of diversity and interdependence: it is good that different individuals have different gifts, and all these different gifts must be orchestrated together for the common good of the community. An important part of the preacher's task will be to discern how these motifs should be balanced to address the needs of the particular local congregation. Some churches, more susceptible to the error of "Lone Ranger" Christianity, may need to hear the appeal for interdependence emphasized, while others, more inclined to press for conformity of Christian experience, may need to hear Paul's affirmation of diverse gifts within the body of Christ. In any case, the image of the body of Christ, as Paul has developed it, provides a vision for authentic community in which there is both great individual freedom (...) and powerful interpersonal sharing and support (...). The goal of our ministry should be nothing less than the formation of such communities.[67]

---

67.   Richard B. Hays, *First Corinthians, Interpretation: A Bible Commentary for Teaching and Preaching* (Louisville, KY: John Knox Press, 1997), p.220.

Every church of which I have been a part has struggled with the diversity of spiritual gifts and the unity we seek. Inevitably, some gifts are more highly valued than others. But that is not Paul's way. Different, yes. Ranked, no. Thus, finding the unity in Christ that God expects of us is always a challenge and requires genuine transformation as a community in the Church.

Stewardship or Trusteeship?

Often, when we speak of our responsibilities of what God has entrusted to us, we speak of our "stewardship." In a sense, we are entrusted with caring for God's household, his family. In Greek, the word for house is *oikos* and the person who oversees the house, who manages it, is called an *oikonomos*. This word is used ten times in the New Testament and is translated variously (based on the context) as steward, or manager, or treasurer in the NRSV. Jesus tells a parable about a bad steward (Luke 16:1-13). This is the story of a trusted steward who squanders the property of his master, which was a particularly despicable crime in Jesus' day. The moral of the story is something like this: use what you possess to serve people because everything you have was given you by God!

When writing to a congregation he founded in Corinth, Greece, Paul referred to himself as 16:1-13). and as a steward, is required to be "trustworthy" (1 Corinthians 4:1-2). Peter reminds us that we, the people of God, are to be "good stewards of the manifold grace of God" (1 Peter 4:10). Clearly, Paul and Peter know that their responsibilities to God extended far beyond their possessions.

But theologian Leonard Sweet suggests that "steward" is probably not the best way to think about this responsibility. After all, he asks, who really uses the word anymore, other than to refer to someone you might meet on a cruise ship?![68] Instead, Sweet suggests that trustee is a more meaningful role for us and would be a better translation of the Greek. Many of us have some experience with trusts, trust funds, and the responsibilities held by trustees, even if it is simply a trustee of some sort of family estate or a guardianship. When we think of ourselves as God's trustees, the message of the Bible becomes a little clearer. We are given dominion over God's creation, not so we can rule as a tough or selfish taskmaster, but so we can be effective trustees of God's wealth, managing it wisely, helping it to grow and flourish. God's creation is not ours, we don't own it; rather, we hold it in trust. In a similar

---

68.   Leonard Sweet, "Freely You Have Received, Freely Give: Toward a Post-Tithing, Post-Stewardship, Postmodern Theology of Receiving," November 29, 2016, https://leonardsweet.com/freely-you-have-received/.

way, we hold the Christian faith in trust and we are charged with guarding what has been entrusted to us (1 Timothy 6:20). We, God's people, the body of Christ, the church, have received a treasure, a trust, given by the Holy Spirit (2 Timothy 1:14). This treasure is the truth about God and the proclamation that Jesus is Lord!

Understanding our responsibilities as being those of a trustee turns church fall stewardship campaigns on their heads. I've been in many Sunday school classes when stewardship time rolls around, prompting us to talk about tithing. Pretty soon, somebody would ask the inevitable question—do we tithe on pre-tax or after-tax income?! But this is backwards. It assumes that all the stuff and money we have is ours and the challenge is to figure out how much we want or need to give to God. Do I give 1 percent, 5 percent, or 10 percent? Tithing has a long tradition in the Christian church, but it has always been accompanied by more talk than tithe! You see, tithing is not the best approach or mindset of the truly faithful trustee. Trustees of God's household recognize that everything we have—money, cars, houses, and stuff—is a gift from God. We use what we need and then grow the rest for God. Do we need to keep for our own use 80 percent of what God entrusts to us? 85 percent? 90 percent?

John Wesley understood this. When he was a young man he earned 30 British pounds a year. He figured out that he needed 28 pounds a year to live on and gave two pounds to the church. When his income increased to 50 pounds, he kept 28 and gave 22. When he made 100 pounds a year, he kept 28 and gave 72. Let those who have ears, hear![69]

---

69.   Charles Edward White, "Four Lessons on Money from One of the World's Richest Preachers," *Christian History* 19 (Summer 1988): p.24.

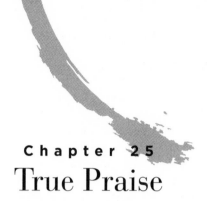

Chapter 25

True Praise

Psalm 150[70]
Praise the LORD! Praise God in his sanctuary; praise him in his mighty fir-mament! Praise him for his mighty deeds; praise him according to his surpass-ing greatness! Praise him with trumpet sound; praise him with lute and harp! Praise him with tambourine and dance; praise him with strings and pipe! Praise him with clanging cymbals; praise him with loud clashing cymbals! Let everything that breathes praise the LORD! Praise the LORD!"

Vocabulary

Preachers and Bible teachers struggle with Christian vocabulary. It isn't that we don't know what the words mean (or at least have our own opinions about their meaning), it's just that we fear being not understood at all or, probably worse, being misunderstood. How do we speak of God and the things of God (theology, that is) to someone who never, rarely, or superfi-cially attends a worship service, or who has never cracked a Bible or been a part of a class? How do we speak in the same sermon or lecture to someone who is only now seeking God and to someone who is a lifelong disciple of our Lord?

Some Christian vocabulary is obviously challenging. Such long-used and nuanced words like atonement, justification, and sanctification, are of-ten avoided rather than taught to laity. Still other so-called "church" words like baptism, salvation, and repentance are used even though many of us might have trouble telling someone what they really mean, at least so far as the body of Christ has long used these words.

But a third category of Christian vocabulary is actually the trickiest of all. These are the words that we hear in worship and in class that we think

---

70. I also recommend reading Psalm 148, which is another enthusiastic call to praise. Since Psalm 150 is the last one in the Psalter, you might also go back and read Psalm 1. You'll see that the order of the psalms is not an accident, but was done with intention.

we know, but we really don't. Love is a good example. In the Christian vocabulary, the best synonym for love is sacrifice. Love is about caring and serving. Love is about what we do, not what we feel. When Jesus says, "love your enemies," he is not so naive as to think that we will have loving feelings toward them. Instead, Jesus calls us to care for and behave toward our enemies as we would our friends and families.

Another word that we think we know but probably don't is praise. Merriam-Webster offers up a definition of praise that probably works for most people: "an expression of approval." We might praise a co-worker who has done a great job or a movie actor for a powerful performance or even a preacher for a well-delivered sermon. Thus, we think that when we speak of praising God, we are speaking or singing our approval of God. God is great. God is the best. God is awesome. And so on.

This is good so far as it goes, but it actually doesn't get us too far. When the writer of the ancient psalms wrote or sang "Praise the LORD!,"[71] he had far more on his heart. Merriam-Webster's has a second definition that gets us closer: to praise is "to glorify". Of course, we are then left wondering what "glorify" really means, though it seems pretty clear that it is more than simply expressing approval. J. Clinton McCann writes, "praise is the offering of one's whole life and self to God."[72] This is far more than an expression of approval or even gratitude. It is far more than a song we might sing or anything we might do in worship. To praise God is to orient our entire life around God. It is to place God at the center of our universe, with ourselves revolving around our Lord. It is to yield to God every moment of every day in all things. It is to submit our will to God's will. It is to acknowledge our dependence upon God – in all things. There can be no part of our lives that is not God's. It is God who is the Master, sovereign over his creation. All this meaning is carried by the seemingly simple word "praise."

To glorify God is to add yet another dimension. In the ancient world, "glory" was a social term. When it was applied to humans in the Old Testament, it was used to show their significance to the world. God's glory is his visible presence. Glory is not a private word; it is a public word. To glorify God is to show the world that God is creator, redeemer, and Lord of all that is. Thus, God's glory is revealed in Jesus. When we behold Christ, we behold God. God's glory is revealed in Jesus' miracles, for they proclaim God's

---

71. In the Hebrew, this line is *Hallelu Yah*. *Hallelu* transliterates the Hebrew word for praise. *Yah* denotes the name of God, as in YHWH, sometimes pronounced Yahweh.
72. J. Clinton McCann, "Psalms" in *NIB*, vol. 4 (Nashville, TN: Abingdon, 1996), p.1279..

work. Similarly, we glorify God with our lives when we live in such a way that God's work can be seen in us.

Now that we've reflected on the meaning of praise, let's take a look at what the psalmist has to say.

Who is to be praised? (v. 1)

The psalmist could not be more straightforward. It is YHWH, the Lord God Almighty, who is to be praised. As Christians, we proclaim that YHWH is eternally Father, Son, and Holy Spirit—personal, social, and one.

Why is God to be praised? (v. 2)

God is to be praised "for his mighty deeds." This is key to understanding God, the biblical view, and Christianity. The God we glorify and proclaim to the world is the God Who Acts. Ours is not a proclamation of philosophies or ideas but of what God has done, is doing, and will do. God creates. God redeems. God sustains. God loves. In all this, God is revealed by his actions, by his mighty deeds. And the deed that reveals the truth about God like no other is Jesus' faithfulness to his vocation—all the way to a cross outside Jerusalem, this loving sacrifice of the Father's son for the sake of the whole world. It is by his deeds that God has revealed to us not only his existence but his character.

How is God to be praised? (v. 3–5)

As we've seen, praise involves every aspect of our life and being. In these verses, the focus is on worship in the temple. There is lots of music (seemingly pretty loud!) and dance. Exuberance might be the right word. Joy and happiness and excitement pouring out. Praise bursting forth. Who could contain it? Indeed, the music is so wonderful and so glorifying that we wonder what could possibly top it, but the psalmist is about to tell us.

Who is to offer the praise? (v. 6)

What can top the temple's orchestra? Only the voices of every creature singing out the praise of God. God breathed life into creation and now God's creatures use that very breath to praise God. McCann writes, "Against this backdrop, Psalm 150 proclaims that the proper goal of every creature is praise—life shaped by God's claim and lived under God's rule.[73] As James L. Mays puts it, "No other use of breath could be more right and true to life than praise of the LORD. No other sound could better speak the gratitude of life than praise of the LORD."[74]

Hallelu Yah! Praise the LORD!

---

73. McCann, p.1279.
74. McCann quotes James Luther Mays from *Psalms: Interpretation: A Bible Commentary for Teaching and Preaching* (Louisville, KY: Westminster John Knox Press, 1994).

PART V

TO LEAD

Let's cut to the quick. We are all called to lead, for leadership in the churches that make up Christ's body cannot be left to a few ordained clergy, full-time staff members, and those willing to volunteer for committees. All believers are called to take the initiative in our common vocation. When someone needs help, it is the task of us all to step up and see that the help is given, even if it doesn't come directly from us. Every growing church on the globe knows the truth of this. I've learned it over the years on occasions too numerous to count. Christians stepping up to lead in even the smallest of tasks, gathering two or three to help. We can never sit and wait for someone else to take the lead. It is in our genuine caring for others that our leadership is seen. Jesus expects this of us; he expects that we will lead in facing every need, in embracing every soul, in leading even strangers to Christ by our actions. How could we be like Jesus, truly embracing our apprenticeship, and yet always wait on others to set the pace? May we all be wise shepherds when needed.

Chapter 26

Lead with
a Servant's Heart

Matthew 20:25–28
*But Jesus called them to him and said, "You know that the rulers of the
Gentiles lord it over them, and their great ones are tyrants over them. It will
not be so among you; but whoever wishes to be great among you must be your
servant, and whoever wishes to be first among you must be your slave; just
as the Son of Man came not to be served but to serve, and to give his life a
ransom for many."*

Hebrews 12:1–3
*Therefore, since we are surrounded by so great a cloud of witnesses, let us also
lay aside every weight and the sin that clings so closely, and let us run with
perseverance the race that is set before us, looking to Jesus the pioneer and per-
fecter of our faith, who for the sake of the joy that was set before him endured
the cross, disregarding its shame, and has taken his seat at the right hand of
the throne of God. Consider him who endured such hostility against himself
from sinners, so that you may not grow weary or lose heart.*

1 Corinthians 10:13
*No testing has overtaken you that is not common to everyone. God is faithful,
and he will not let you be tested beyond your strength, but with the testing he
will also provide the way out so that you may be able to endure it.*

What Kind of Leader Are You?

We are all asked to lead. Sometimes in a large organization. Sometimes
in a small group. Among a group of friends. Or in our family. All of us are
called upon to influence the behavior and thinking of other people with
whom we are seeking a shared goal. Leadership is inescapable. We all lead
and we all are led.

Jesus led.[75] In leadership-speak, Jesus formed a team, showed them a vision of where they were headed, and taught them how to get there in everything he said and did. But even for Jesus, leading wasn't easy. His disciples were often confused, blind to the larger picture, unable to understand or live out what Jesus was trying to teach them – at least until after Jesus was gone. For then, over the next decades, Jesus' disciples, now apostles, spread across the Mediterranean world, building for the kingdom of God.

Ken Blanchard, of *The One Minute Manager*[76] fame, set out to learn more about Jesus' leadership from the four gospel accounts. Blanchard writes, "I soon became aware that everything I had ever taught or written about effective leadership during the past thirty-five years, Jesus did to perfection, beyond my ability to portray or describe."[77] Perhaps so. It is certainly a provocative claim, but may neglect the distinctiveness of the Church and the work of the Holy Spirit in a world filled with people who are at best apathetic and, at worst, hostile to God as revealed in Jesus Christ. Still, we can learn a great deal about leadership from Jesus. We just have to be ready to be surprised—as surprised as the disciples.

Wishing to Serve

Jesus' leadership began with the heart, not the head, not even the hands. A humble heart. A giving heart. A serving heart. The passage from Matthew is taken from the last days before Jesus' crucifixion. Two disciples, the brothers James and John,[78] the sons of Zebedee, get their mom to go to Jesus and ask that her sons be elevated among the group so that they can sit at Jesus' right and left hands in the kingdom.[79] When the other disciples hear what has happened, they are understandably upset and go to Jesus, who seizes the teaching moment. The Gentiles may lord it over one another, Jesus says, each seeking to rise higher than the next, but that is not to be the way of Jesus' disciples. They are to emulate Jesus, remembering that they are to serve, not be served.

75. Jesus was led as well, as he sought to follow his Father's will in living out the vocation given him by his Father. Jesus prayed at nearly every turn in the gospels. Great leaders also know how to follow well.

76. Ken Blanchard and Spencer Johnson, *The One Minute Manager* (New York, NY: William Morrow, 1982).

77. Ken Blanchard and Phil Hodges, *Lead Like Jesus: Lessons for Everyone from the Greatest Leadership Role Model of All Time* (Nashville, TN: Thomas Nelson, 2005), p.xi.

78. New Testament names can be confusing. This James did not write the book of James in your New Testament; that was the half-brother of Jesus. Nor is it likely that this John wrote the gospel of John. Keep in mind, 41.5% of Palestinian Jewish males (as opposed to Jews living outside Palestine) bore one of nine names, hence the problem of potential confusion.

79. It wasn't unusual for Mediterranean mothers to seek status and prestige for and through their sons. Here again we see at work a culture built around honor and shame.

Such discipleship and servant leadership isn't about being nice or even helpful. It is about putting the interests of others ahead of our own (see Philippians 2:1–11), even when that means substantial sacrifices from us. Blanchard writes, "A heart motivated by self-interest looks at the world as a 'give a little, take a lot' proposition. People with hearts motivated by self-interest put their agenda, safety, status, and gratification ahead of that of those affected by their thoughts and actions."[80] The question Blanchard asks is pretty much the same question Jesus asks the brothers James and John: Are you a self-serving leader or a servant leader?

Likewise, the writer of Hebrews, sometimes referred to as the Preacher, points us toward the example of Christ. Even when we tire or lose heart, we are to, as John West puts it, "keep on keepin' on"[81] for Christ, our model and our hope. Jesus endures setting aside humiliation and shame, always keeping his eye and his heart on the goal (again, back to Philippians 2:1–11).

EGO

Ken Blanchard and Phil Hodges have a clever way of creating helpful acronyms such as their explanation of EGO.[82] For example, they ask whether our ego gets in the way of our faithful obedience. Does our EGO "Edge God Out?" Do we allow ourselves to be driven by pride and fear? Pride pushes us toward the promotion of ourselves, at the expense of others. Fear pushes us toward the protection of ourselves, again at the expense of others. In their self-promotion before Jesus, the brothers James and John reveal their prideful desire for status and recognition. Or —will we seek an EGO that "Exalts God Only"? Will we embrace a life built on humility rather than pride, and confidence rather than fear?

Blanchard suggests that trading one EGO in for the other is a matter of

- embracing an eternal perspective;[83]
- seeking to lead for a higher purpose;
- carefully assessing our own faith and trust in God; and
- seeking the guidance of the Holy Spirit.[84]

80. Blanchard and Hodges. p.40.
81. Lyric from the John West song, "Highway to Roppongi" from the album *Long Time, No Sing*, 2006.
82. Blanchard and Hodges. p.40.
83. Your life is more than the time between your birth and your death and it is larger than the world you can see and touch right now. Christians are to have a very expansive view of God's reality.
84. Blanchard and Hodges. p.63-64.

All this is sound advice that has been taught and modeled by Christians for two thousand years.

Blanchard and Hodges even suggest a twelve step program to move from "Edge God Out" to "Exalt God Only" patterned on Alcoholics Anonymous![85] That may seem a tad too clever, but Blanchard and Hodges are right to see that many of us have nurtured egos that get in the way of our discipleship and joy. Perhaps, a twelve-step EGO Anonymous program actually would help.

Community

Paul's aphorism from 1 Corinthians 10:13 can be puzzling. Really? God won't allow me to be tested with more than I can handle? I can certainly imagine events in my life that I'm not at all confident I could handle. Trading in one ego for another won't insulate me from suffering and problems.

But it is important to know Paul isn't really speaking to "me." The "yous" here are plural. Paul is speaking to the community not to any one individual. It is in community that we learn to "Exalt God Only." It is in fellowship that we learn the way of forgiveness and grace. Together, we learn how to lead with servants' hearts. And in all this, God is forever faithful. Paul Sampley writes, "With every test, the faithful, dependable God will make sure it is something you can collectively handle, or God will provide an exodus as in olden times."[86] Amen.

For a Deeper Understanding

Lead Like Jesus

Ken Blanchard and Spencer Johnson's *The One Minute Manager* has remained one of the most popular books on managing people in organizations. A reviewer on Amazon wrote, "For an adult to have not read this book, to me, is like a person who never read *Green Eggs & Ham* or 'Jack and Jill.'" That may be a bit of overstatement, but there is no denying that *The One Minute Manager* is one of the best-selling and enduring business books of all time.

Ken Blanchard recounts how, after the phenomenal success of his first book, he began to feel God's pull. It took a long time, but Blanchard even-

---

85. Blanchard and Hodges. p.71

86. J. Paul Sampley, "2nd Corinthians," in *NIB*, vol. 10 (Nashville, TN: Abingdon, 1999), p.916.

tually turned his life over to Jesus. Being a behavioral scientist, Blanchard found himself reading the gospels with an eye to Jesus' leadership style and methods. The result of his reading was the popular book, *Lead Like Jesus*, which he wrote with a long-time friend, Phil Hodges.[87] This book too has proven to be popular.

The Letter to the Hebrews

Other than Revelation, no book of the New Testament seems more foreign to most Christian readers than the Letter to the Hebrews. And the reason is clear. More than any other New Testament book, Hebrews is steeped in the Old Testament world of temples, priests, and sacrifice. Since most of us don't know much about the Old Testament, we are puzzled by the writer's theology, illustrations, and allusions. Our understanding is made all the more difficult because we can't answer the simplest questions about the letter: Who wrote it? When? To whom? In his commentary on Hebrews, scholar Thomas G. Long gives us a good and colorful sense of the problems:

> Among the books of the New Testament, the epistle to the Hebrews stands out as both strange and fascinating. Unique in style and content, as a piece of literature it is simply unlike any of the other epistles. Though some of its phrases are among the best-known and most often quoted passages in the New Testament, many contemporary Christians are largely unacquainted with the book as a whole, finding themselves lost in its serpentine passageways and elaborate theological arguments.[88]

For those who take ropes, spikes, and torches and descend into the murky cave of Hebrews, there is much about this document we wish we could discover, but our historical lanterns are too dim. For example, we wish we knew who wrote this curious epistle. Even though many names have been suggested—Apollos, Barnabas, Luke, Clement of Rome, Priscilla, and Silvanus, to mention a few—the arguments are not strong for any particular candidate. We actually have a firmer grasp of who did not write Hebrews than who did, since on stylistic grounds alone, it is a virtual certainty that the apostle Paul did not pen this letter. But who did? The best answer to that question is the comment attributed to Christian theologian Origen of Alexandria in the third century: "But who wrote the epistle, in truth God knows."

---

87. Blanchard and Hodges.
88. Thomas G. Long, *Hebrews, Interpretation: A Bible Commentary for Teaching and Preaching* (Louisville, KY: Westminster John Knox Press, 1997), p.1-2.

We also wish we knew more than we do about the recipients, the first readers. Were they in Rome? Jerusalem? Colossae? Were they Gentiles? Jews? A mixture? We can only guess at the answers to these questions. The one current geographical reference in the book, which mentions Italy, is ambiguous (see comment on 13:24). Early on, someone attached a title to the text—To the Hebrews—but whoever did that was probably just speculating about its original recipients and was as much in the dark as we are.

Moreover, we would like to be able to pinpoint the date Hebrews was written, but we can only provide an approximate timeframe. Clement of Rome appears to quote Hebrews in a letter written sometime near the end of the first century, so it had to be composed before then. Also, most scholars believe that the elaborate Christology of Hebrews could not have developed overnight and would more likely reflect the theological activity of the second or third generation of Christians. Putting these thoughts and a few other bits and pieces of evidence together, most scholars make an educated guess of A.D. 60 to 100 as the possible span during which Hebrews was composed.

So we peer into the depths of the text unsure of who wrote it, to whom, from where, or when. Imagine being handed a book today with the comment, "Here, you may enjoy this. It was written in America or Russia or France, I'm not sure, by a Jew—or was it a Gentile?—anyway, it was written sometime between 1920 and 1970. Enjoy."

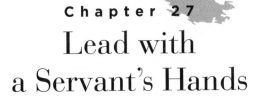

Chapter 27

Lead with a Servant's Hands

Matthew 4:18-22

As he walked by the Sea of Galilee, he saw two brothers, Simon, who is called Peter, and Andrew his brother, casting a net into the sea—for they were fishermen. And he said to them, "Follow me, and I will make you fish for people." Immediately they left their nets and followed him. As he went from there, he saw two other brothers, James son of Zebedee and his brother John, in the boat with their father Zebedee, mending their nets, and he called them. Immediately they left the boat and their father, and followed him.

Matthew 9:35–38

Then Jesus went about all the cities and villages, teaching in their synagogues, and proclaiming the good news of the kingdom, and curing every disease and every sickness. When he saw the crowds, he had compassion for them, because they were harassed and helpless, like sheep without a shepherd. Then he said to his disciples, "The harvest is plentiful, but the laborers are few; therefore ask the Lord of the harvest to send out laborers into his harvest."

John 17:1–4

After Jesus had spoken these words, he looked up to heaven and said, "Father the hour has come; glorify your Son so that the Son may glorify you, since you have given him authority over all people, to give eternal life to all whom you have given him. And this is eternal life, that they may know you, the only true God, and Jesus Christ whom you have sent. I glorified you on earth by finishing the work that you gave me to do."

Do as I Do

Jesus led with his hands not just his words. He lived out the reality of the kingdom of God. Do we lead with our hands? Do we lead like Jesus?[89]

People are surprised when they find out that I do not recommend using a red-letter Bible, in which Jesus' words, and nothing else, are highlighted in red ink. It's not that I'm against Jesus' teachings; the problem is that a red-letter Bible makes it seem that what Jesus did was less important than what he said. Yet, we know from our own experiences that what we do often reveals more about who we are than what we say. Even our children know that the ole' adage, "Do as I say, not as I do" is problematic, if not hypocritical. They will call us out, too. Jesus had the wisdom as a teacher to both say it and do it.

And what did Jesus do? He traveled and he taught. He proclaimed the arrival of the kingdom of God and he invited and he welcomed—and he healed. All of this was focused on Jesus' astonishing claim that in him, the long-awaited dawning of God's kingdom had arrived. As Jesus puts it in the opening of Mark's gospel, "The time is fulfilled, the kingdom of God is at hand; repent, and believe in the good news" (Mark 1:15).

It is pretty easy for us to grasp that Jesus taught about the kingdom of God. Many of Jesus' parables begin with the phrase, "The kingdom of God is like . . . ."[90] The Sermon on the Mount is an extended teaching of what the kingdom of God is like. But let's also look at Jesus' actions. He dined with tax collectors and prostitutes. He healed the lame and the blind and the sick. Yes, these were acts of compassion, but they were far more: they were enactments of the kingdom of God. Jesus' actions were not just mini-dramas to make a point, but the genuine bursting forth of God's kingdom.

Consider Jesus' announcement of his ministry in Luke 4. Jesus rises to speak in the Nazareth synagogue and reads from the scroll of Isaiah: "The Spirit of the Lord is upon me, because he has appointed me to bring good news to the poor. He has sent me to proclaim release to the captives and recovery of sight to the blind, to let the oppressed go free, to proclaim the year of the Lord's favor" (v. 18-19).

When Jesus fed the poor, healed the sick, made the blind see and the rest, he was showing people that God's kingdom had arrived. Jesus was showing that in God's kingdom there is no hunger and no sickness and no

89. Blanchard and Hodges.
90. Being sensitive to some Jews' refusal even to say the word God, Matthew uses "kingdom of heaven" rather than "kingdom of God," but they mean the same thing.

blindness. Again, these were not merely live-action parables. It was more like Jesus was opening a portal[91] into the kingdom of God when he cured each sick person.

The reality of God's kingdom and its arrival 2,000 years ago is what makes Christian mission work different than it appears to some. Whether it is feeding the hungry, providing mosquito nets to offset malaria, or proclaiming the Good News, all of these are also enactments of God's kingdom, portals into a world without hunger, malaria, or ignorance.

A full belly may look like no more than a full belly to some—but there is far more going on. It is a bit like seeing a Bible sitting on a table. For many, the Bible is no more than a marginally interesting collection of ancient writings. But, in truth, the Bible is much more than that. It is the "God-breathed" revelation of God's self. It is the God-given testimony to Jesus Christ, the living Word of God. As the cliché goes, there is more to the Bible than meets the eye. And there is more to each act of compassion of Christ.

A Leader's Hand

In the kingdom of God, leaders serve. Each time we put the interests of others ahead of our own, each time we help those in need, each time we set aside our prideful ambition, we are building the kingdom of God. This is not only what servant leaders say, but also what they do. It is what Jesus did. But how do we learn to be a serving leader? How do we set aside the world's conceptions and our own ambitions about what it means to be a leader?

Blanchard and Hodges remind us that Jesus's disciples were complete novices when he first called to them at the seaside. Jesus took them from novices to teachers and leaders in their own right, able with the help of God's Holy Spirit, to build a church that endures to this day.

Likewise, we have to learn to be servant leaders. Each of us begins as a novice, or as Peter puts it, a newborn infant feeding on the "pure, spiritual milk," so that we might "grow into salvation" (1 Peter 2:2). We learn to be trustworthy apprentices, eager for, as Paul puts it, "solid food" (1 Corin-

---

91. The kingdom of God is not merely a conception of our heads or hearts. It is real; every bit as real as the pavement you and I walk on each day. The best way to think about God's kingdom is as a parallel reality that will one day fully wash over our own. The coming of the kingdom is not about our going somewhere, it is about that somewhere being fully here. One of the things I like about the Harry Potter series is that it opens its readers to the possibility of two parallel realities, the world of wizards and the world of muggles, which somehow coexist in the same "space." One world is fully aware of the other, while one lives in near ignorance of the other.

thians 3:2). We strive to be maturing and ever-growing disciples of Jesus Christ.

But of course, God doesn't stop with us there. We are to be disciples with a purpose, modeling Christ with our heart, hands, head, and habits. In this sense, we are all missionaries. It is this outward focus that is so easy for us to forget. It is not just about helping out or doing good for others. It is about proclaiming the Good News in all that we say and do. Freeing the oppressed, healing the sick, feeding the poor—this is not just Jesus' work; it is our work too. And every moment spent doing such work is a moment lived within the kingdom of God.

For a Deeper Understanding

Lesslie Newbigin

Lesslie Newbigin was arguably one of the most influential missionary theologians of the late twentieth-century. After finishing his Oxford studies for ordination, Newbigin and his wife, Helen, set sail for India where they would serve in the mission field for the next 35 years. After his so-called retirement, Bishop Newbigin provided leadership to mission agencies and efforts around the globe, though his most lasting influence has been in Europe and America, which Newbigin came to see as mission fields in themselves. Tim Stafford writes:

> Ministry in England, he discovered, "is much harder than anything I met in India. There is a cold contempt for the Gospel which is harder to face than opposition. . . .England is a pagan society and the development of a truly missionary encounter with this very tough form of paganism is the greatest intellectual and practical task facing the Church."
>
> From that rude confrontation with pagan England has come an outpouring of books and lectures. Newbigin looked at the West with a missionary's eye and asked a missionary's analytic questions. How can we evangelize this culture, built on Christian foundations yet utterly unwilling to consider (almost unable to understand) the Christian's claim to know the truth that will set us free? It is hard, Newbigin knew, for a Hindu or a Muslim to come to worship Christ. For an Englishman, it would seem, it had become even harder.[92]

Newbigin is always worth reading. Recently, Paul Weston pulled together an anthology of Bishop Newbigin's writings.[93]

92. Tim Stafford, "God's Missionary to Us, Part 1," *Christianity Today*, Dec. 9, 1996.
93. Paul Weston, ed. *Lesslie Newbigin, Missionary Theologian: A Reader* (Grand Rapids,

What Is the Church's Mission?

What exactly is the church's mission in this world? Preaching the word? Making disciples? Feeding the poor? Regrettably, Christians have too often seen these as competing choices. But a better understanding of what Jesus meant by the kingdom of God would go a long way to leading us out of this particular trap of false choices. In an interview in *Christianity Today*, Bishop N. T. Wright was asked to talk about the church's mission:

> For generations the church has been polarized between those who see the main task being the saving of souls for heaven and the nurturing of those souls through the valley of this dark world on the one hand, and on the other hand those who see the task of improving the lot of human beings and the world, rescuing the poor from their misery.
>
> The longer that I've gone on as a New Testament scholar and wrestled with what the early Christians were actually talking about, the more it's been borne in on me that that distinction is one that we modern Westerners bring to the text rather than finding in the text. Because the great emphasis in the New Testament is that the gospel is not how to escape the world; the gospel is that the crucified and risen Jesus is the Lord of the world. And that his death and Resurrection transform the world, and that transformation can happen to you. You, in turn, can be part of the transforming work.... When I lecture about this, people will pop up and say, "Surely Jesus said my kingdom is not of this world." And the answer is no, what Jesus said in John 18 is, "My kingdom is not from this world." That's *ek tou kosmoutoutou*. It's quite clear in the text that Jesus' kingdom doesn't start with this world. It isn't a worldly kingdom, but it is for this world. It's from somewhere else, but it's for this world.[94]

There's a fine point here. We do not build the kingdom of God; that is God's work. But, we can build for the kingdom. We must do all we can, empowered by the Holy Spirit, to make God's love and justice manifest in this world, to make concrete what seems like mere sentiment to so many. We proclaim the gospel and we strive to meet the very real needs of everyday people. There is no choice. It is one of those "ands" that marks the Christian faith; it can never be an "or." Jesus expects nothing less.

We want to make the choice. We want it crystal clear. Black or white. Saving souls (as if we could) or feeding the hungry. But we must resist the choice; Jesus calls us to both. We are to be his witnesses to the ends of the

MI: Eerdmans, 2006).
94. N. T. Wright, quoted in an interview with Tim Stafford, "Mere Mission," *Christianity Today*, Jan. 5, 2007.

earth (Acts 1) and we are to feed the hungry, clothe the naked, welcome the stranger, and so on (Matthew 25:31-46). This is the life of a disciple, nothing less.

Chapter 28

Lead with a Servant's Head

John 13:12–15

After he had washed their feet, had put on his robe, and had returned to the table, he said to them, "Do you know what I have done to you? You call me Teacher and Lord—and you are right, for that is what I am. So, if I, your Lord and Teacher, have washed your feet, you also ought to wash one another's feet. For I have set you an example, that you also should do as I have done to you."

Habakkuk 2:1–4

I will stand at my watchpost, and station myself on the rampart; I will keep watch to see what he will say to me, and what he will answer concerning my complaint. Then the LORD answered me and said: Write the vision; make it plain on tablets, so that a runner may read it. For there is still a vision for the appointed time; it speaks of the end, and does not lie. If it seems to tarry, wait for it; it will surely come, it will not delay.

Vision

What does it mean to see the world through Jesus' eyes? How do we embrace this vision once grasped and how do we lead others to embrace it as well?

Vision and leader: the two words go together. Many people would be skeptical that the words servant and leader go together, but vision and leader, you betcha. In their book, *Lead Like Jesus*, Ken Blanchard and Phil Hodges present Ken and Jesse Stoner's three-part framework of what makes a compelling vision:

1. Your purpose. What business are you in? Where are you going and why? Or in terms of your family, what is your family all about? Where is your family going and why?

2. Your picture of the future. What will your future look like if you are accomplishing your purpose?

3. Your values. What do you stand for? On what principles will you make ongoing decisions?"[95]

This is all good stuff and you can certainly see all three at work in Jesus' leadership. Jesus understood his purpose and stayed committed to it even though it led to a horrifying death. Jesus certainly had a clear picture of the future. No rose-colored glasses for him; Jesus knew the confrontation to which he was leading his disciples. And, of course, Jesus also grasped the bigger picture, the promise that the day of salvation was arriving in him and his God-given vocation. Thirdly, Jesus taught about the kingdom of God, kingdom values we might call them, in much of what he said and did.

Yet, —and it is always a big puzzling yet for me—Jesus' disciples, those who spent the most time with him, remained largely blind to all this. There are many examples we could look at, for the disciples' blindness is a large theme in the synoptic[96] gospels. Here are a few examples:

Though Peter eventually names Jesus as "the Messiah, the son of the living God" (Matthew 16:16), soon thereafter Peter cannot yet comprehend that Jesus' vocation will take him to his death. Peter even tempts Jesus with avoiding it, as if Jesus needed any more temptation to turn away from such a horrible path (Matthew 16:21–23).

Right before Jesus' triumphal entry into Jerusalem, some disciples jockeyed for privileged positions (Matthew 20:25–28).

And, of course, Peter's three-time denial and the disciples' abandonment of Jesus when he is arrested by the authorities.[97]

The disciples just never seem to get it, and the question that has always troubled me is "Why?" How could I, living in Texas 2,000 years later, ever hope to "get it"? Admittedly, I take some comfort in the disciples' obtuse-

95. Blanchard and Hodges.
96. The synoptic gospels are Matthew, Mark, and Luke. All three share the same basic story line and even some material. These similarities gave rise to their being called synoptic, which means "seen side by side."
97. The examples could fill a book. I've always thought that one of the best evidences of the gospels' authenticity is the obtuse blindness of the disciples. Since it is their story to tell after Jesus' death and resurrection, why would they come off so badly at times unless the gospel portraits are accurate.

ness, as it makes me feel better about my own weaknesses. Yet, I'm still left wondering why the disciples couldn't see and asking myself what it means for my faith, my discipleship, and my own leadership.

Why wasn't Jesus able to bring his closest disciples to the place they would be after his death, resurrection, and ascension: preaching with great power and courage?[98] Might Jesus simply have been a poor leader, unable to communicate in word or deed the vision that he wanted to share with his disciples? That thought seems at least mildly blasphemous, but still the question remains.

Swapping Glasses

Perhaps we are confused by the disciples' blindness because we underestimate the enormity of the change laid before them. And, in the same way, we underestimate the transformation entailed when we come to faith in Jesus Christ.

The image of the disciples being blind is a good one, for it draws us to the question of vision. I'm not speaking merely of where we are going or even where we are now. It is a question of seeing things as they really are, seeing the true nature of reality, looking through right-seeing glasses.

The disciples had a particular worldview. Jesus had a worldview. You and I have worldviews. A worldview consists of our answers to the most basic questions of life. A worldview is our understanding of how the world works. If you are ever in an argument with someone and things reach the point where the person exclaims in exasperation, "Well, that's just how things are!" you've run right into their worldview.

The disciples lived within the world of second-temple Judaism. They lived under the thumb of the Romans while awaiting the day when God would finally step in and put things right, when God would keep all the glorious promises found in the writings of the prophets. And, as typical second-temple Jews, the disciples just knew that this great day would be ushered in by the arrival of God's right-hand man, the Messiah, who would swoop in with power and might and wonder and glory. Everyone would see it, even the hated Romans.

Consequently, Jesus didn't just want his disciples to see more clearly. Jesus needed them to swap one pair of glasses for another, one way of seeing and being for another. He wanted them to adopt a wholly new worldview,

---

98. Somewhere in here there is perhaps a clue to what Jesus meant when, on the eve of his crucifixion, he said it was to the disciples' advantage that he leave, for otherwise, the Spirit could not come to them. (See John 16:7.)

to see that God's saving power would be manifested in sacrifice and faithfulness, not power and might and wonder. We fail to grasp the gospels if we fail to grasp the radical swapping of worldviews required to see the truth about Jesus.

This is in large part what Paul means when he writes, "Do not be conformed to this world, but be transformed by the renewing of your minds, so that you may discern what is the will of God—what is good and acceptable and perfect" (Romans 12:2).

This mind-renewing, glasses-swapping transformation can be as difficult for us as it was for the disciples. Today we think we know how the world works when we really don't. We think we are seeing the truth when we are not. Indeed, again like the disciples, were it not for the work of the Holy Spirit, we would never be able to see the world as it really is. And even with the Spirit's help, it still takes training and time to grow into our new glasses.

A Leader's Vision

Written during the final decades of Jerusalem before its demise at the hands of the Babylonians, the Old Testament book of Habakkuk[99] focuses on a problem we all share. How can we believe that things will really be put right in a world filled with so much wrong? Or to put it another way, how do we really trust in God's justice when the world is so obviously unjust?

The vision given to Habakkuk is a guarantee that God will put things right, that God's saving justice will remake all of creation. And we are to trust that God will do what God has promised to do ("the righteous live by their faith," v. 4).

But still, that doesn't answer all our questions. We do live in an unjust world, filled with wrongs and tragedies. What is to be our response? How do we really live by faith? In his commentary on this Habakkuk passage in *The New Interpreter's Bible*, Theodore Hiebert writes:

> The righteous, the sincerely religious, those who long and work for justice and righteousness receive the strength to go on, not because the world itself is just or because it rewards those who work for justice, but because these persons possess a larger vision of the way things should be. They possess the vision, as did Habakkuk, of God's just reign.[100]

---

99. Tucked away in the back of your Old Testament are the books of the twelve so-called "minor" or "lesser" prophets. The tag "minor" refers only to the length of the writings, not to the prophets' message or importance. The book of Habakkuk is one of the twelve.

100. Theodore Hiebert, "Habakkuk," in *NIB*, vol. 7 (Nashville, TN: Abingdon Press,

This is the question we need to ask ourselves: "Do I possess the vision of God's just reign?" Jesus tried to help his disciples to see the truth of God's just reign, i.e., the kingdom of God. He wanted them to see that contrary to the way they thought the world worked, the words servant and leader actually do go together. Yes, the Messiah would wash their feet.

I've come to believe that our transformation into the people God desires us to be entails a massive change in the way we see things. The key is to see that God's just reign is not just about the future, it is also about the present. Two thousand years ago, Jesus of Nazareth ushered in God's just reign, this kingdom of God, and it is not just in our hearts, it is reality.

Philip Yancey writes about the "rumors of another world" in a book by that title[101] and he is right, there is another world every bit as real as the keyboard on which I am typing this book. Just because I can't see it, doesn't make it less real.

Learning to see God and God's reign in all things won't happen overnight. But if we are going to lead like Jesus, we have to commit ourselves fully to the transformation of our vision. You might begin simply. When you watch a movie, ask yourself what the movie had to say about ourselves, this world—about God. This goes for any movie, not just the obviously God-oriented ones. What worldview is the movie presenting? How closely does it align with a Christian worldview? The world wants to shape us into its mold; God wants to shape us into Jesus' mold. Whose glasses will we wear?

1996).

101. Philip Yancey, *Rumors of Another World: What on Earth Are We Missing?* (Grand Rapids, MI: Zondervan, 2003).

Lead With
a Servant's Habits

Matthew 26:36–41

Then Jesus went with them to a place called Gethsemane; and he said to his disciples, "Sit here while I go over there and pray." He took with him Peter and the two sons of Zebedee, and began to be grieved and agitated. Then he said to them, "I am deeply grieved, even to death; remain here, and stay awake with me." And going a little farther, he threw himself on the ground and prayed, "My Father, if it is possible, let this cup pass from me; yet not what I want but what you want." Then he came to the disciples and found them sleeping; and he said to Peter, "So, could you not stay awake with me one hour? Stay awake and pray that you may not come into the time of trial; the spirit indeed is willing, but the flesh is weak."

Psalm 46:1–5, 10–11

God is our refuge and strength, a very present help in trouble. Therefore, we will not fear, though the earth should change, though the mountains shake in the heart of the sea; though its waters roar and foam, though the mountains tremble with its tumult. There is a river whose streams make glad the city of God, the holy habitation of the Most High. God is in the midst of the city; it shall not be moved; God will help it when the morning dawns. "Be still, and know that I am God! I am exalted among the nations, I am exalted in the earth." The LORD of hosts is with us; the God of Jacob is our refuge.

What Lies Ahead

How do we prepare ourselves for what lies ahead? How do we become servant leaders? What habits shape us into the leaders God would have us be?

The rocky Garden of Gethsemane was the place of testing, temptation, and submission. Jesus came there to pray on the eve of his crucifixion. He prayed for strength and even for another way forward, a way to avoid the horror that he knew lay just ahead. Avoiding the cross would be easy. Escape out the back of the garden, down the backside of the Mount of Olives, and into the Judean wilderness, where no one could be found unless they wanted to be found. But Jesus prayed in the Garden and Jesus stayed. He found the strength to remain faithful to the work that God had given him. He found the discipline to resist temptation, to turn aside from the easy way out.

We will all face a Gethsemane of one sort or another during our lives. Some big, some small. They are times of testing and crisis. The question is how we will respond. Will it be in faith or in panic? In confidence or in terror? Even more to the point, will we stand or will we run? How can we prepare ourselves for the difficult times that await us, so that we can remain faithful and hopeful, knowing—knowing!—that, as the psalmist wrote, "God is our refuge and strength, a very present help in trouble" (Psalm 46:1).

The Habits of Crisis

Reflecting on how we could possibly learn to respond to crisis as Jesus responded in the Garden of Gethsemane brought to mind my pilot training days in the Air Force. I had a low draft lottery number. (If you are young enough to have no clue what I'm talking about, be grateful.) So, I went into the ROTC in college and entered the USAF upon graduation where I spent my first twelve months learning to fly jets.

A key part of the Air Force. curriculum was learning what to do in the event of an emergency, like the loss of one or both engines. We had manuals telling us what to do and classroom instruction on every conceivable problem. We wore a quick-flip book of emergency procedures strapped to our thigh every time we went up. Our instructor pilots would demonstrate for us and then we'd practice and practice and then practice some more, until we got past the panic and grew confident. Over time, we knew what to do, so much so, that we'd hardly have to think about it, and only act.

For 2,000 years Jesus' followers have "practiced" their faith, endeavoring to deepen their trust in God, to renew and transform their minds, to serve others, and to prepare themselves for the storms of life. We practice and we practice and we practice again.

On his return trip from America, John Wesley's ship was overrun by a storm that caused Wesley to fear for his life. In the midst of the tumult, he observed the serenity of some of his fellow travelers, a group of Moravian pietists[102]. He saw in them a deep and abiding faith, a peace in the face of terrible events that he desired for himself.

Though such faith is certainly a gift from God, it must also be learned and cultivated by being totally immersed in God and the ways of God. The spiritual disciplines are long-tested means of helping in this immersion, preparing us for the inevitable crises so that they do not overwhelm.

Likewise, learning to be a servant takes practice, or as I said earlier, training not merely trying. Prayer, reflective Scripture reading, worship, Bible study, and service each help to develop within us the habits of a servant. It is a bit like language training. Anyone who has tried to learn a second language knows that nothing beats total immersion in the new language. So also, the habits of servanthood are best learned by immersion.

I was a bit surprised toward the end of Blanchard and Hodges' book *Lead Like Jesus*. Their chapter on the habits of a servant leader has none of the leadership-speak, no tips on the practices of effective leaders, no more principles for the servant leader to follow. Instead, they turn to reflections on prayer, meditation, Scripture memorization, and reading of the Bible. They speak of intimacy in relationships, the importance of group accountability, and listening to those who would dare tell us the truth. All of this points to the need to embrace the total transformation of ourselves. The spiritual disciplines are essential to this extreme makeover.

So this is where my guidance on servant leadership ends and your practice of it begins. These disciplines help us to become like Jesus, to love like Jesus, and to lead like Jesus.

For a Deeper Understanding

A Tale of Two Gardens

Adam was once in a garden. He had the opportunity to be obedient, to trust that God knows best and, thus, refuse to eat the fruit of the forbidden tree. But Adam did not trust. He was not obedient. He came to his time of testing and trial—and failed. His disobedience set in motion the wrecking of humanity's relationship with God and the distortion of all creation.

Jesus, on the other hand, came to a garden on that spring night in 30AD. Like Adam, Jesus also had his obedience tested. The gospel accounts of Jesus' Gethsemane experience reveal a man struggling with his choice,

---

102.   German (Moravian) pietism is a movement within the Lutheran Church that emphasizes individual piety in Christian living and not doctrine alone. The movement dates to the 17th century.

struggling to be obedient to his father. But where Adam failed, Jesus succeeded. And in this lies our salvation.

The Garden of Gethsemane is the reversal of the Garden of Eden. Jesus' decision to remain faithful in his obedience, to press on to the cross, was the means for the healing of relationship and the restoration of the cosmos. As Paul wrote in his letter to the Romans, "For just as by the one man's disobedience the many were made sinners, so by the one man's obedience the many will be made righteous" (Romans 5:19).

Despite our proclamation that Jesus was fully divine and fully human, we sometimes tend to cloud over his humanity. We have trouble imagining that Jesus was truly fearful or anxious, as if the right question is, "How could God be scared?" But that's not the right question. Instead, we must strive to resist the temptation to see Jesus as less than human. Jesus faced the temptations and trials we face. For as Douglas Hare writes, "If Jesus was not fully human, the cross was an empty pantomime."[103]

103.   Douglas R. A. Hare, *Matthew: Interpretation: A Bible Commentary for Teaching and Preaching* (Louisville, KY: Westminster John Knox Press, 1993). p.300.

Chapter 30

Knowing What You Have While You Have It

Matthew 21:33–46

"Listen to another parable. There was a landowner who planted a vineyard, put a fence around it, dug a wine press in it, and built a watchtower. Then he leased it to tenants and went to another country. When the harvest time had come, he sent his slaves to the tenants to collect his produce. But the tenants seized his slaves and beat one, killed another, and stoned another. Again, he sent other slaves, more than the first; and they treated them in the same way. Finally, he sent his son to them, saying, 'They will respect my son.' But when the tenants saw the son, they said to themselves, 'This is the heir; come, let us kill him and get his inheritance.' So they seized him, threw him out of the vineyard, and killed him. Now when the owner of the vineyard comes, what will he do to those tenants?" They said to Jesus, "He will put those wretches to a miserable death, and lease the vineyard to other tenants who will give him the produce at the harvest time." Jesus said to them, "Have you never read in the scriptures: 'The stone that the builders rejected has become the cornerstone; this was the Lord's doing, and it is amazing in our eyes'?[104] Therefore I tell you, the kingdom of God will be taken away from you and given to a people that produces the fruits of the kingdom. The one who falls on this stone will be broken to pieces; and it will crush anyone on whom it falls." When the chief priests and the Pharisees heard his parables, they realized that he was speaking about them. They wanted to arrest him, but they feared the crowds, because they regarded him as a prophet.

How easy it is to take for granted the gifts and blessings that we have or even never see to them for what they are. This story is about some leaders who not only failed to see how God was working in their midst, but even turned against God in their blindness.

The parables certainly drive home the importance of looking at the context when we strive to hear Jesus' meaning. This parable is part of an ex-

---

104.   From Psalm 118:22–23. This parable is also attributed to Jesus in Acts 4:11 and 1 Peter 2:7.

tended confrontation between Jesus and the Jewish leadership, represented by the temple priests and the Pharisees. Jesus arrives in Jerusalem to adoring crowds on a Sunday (Matthew 21), which we celebrate as Palm Sunday. The first thing Jesus does after his arrival is to head for the temple, where he invokes the words and actions of the prophet Jeremiah, who, 600 years before, had his own confrontation with the temple leadership. The next morning, Jesus returns to the temple where the "chief priests and elders" question his authority. Whose authority underlies Jesus' words and actions? The leaders know full well that Jesus says and does only what God would say and do and they want to know from what or from whom Jesus claims his authority.

Jesus replies to this challenge by turning the tables and asking the chief priests and elders a question that they refuse to answer: "Who authorized the baptisms performed by John the Baptizer: heaven or humans?"[105] Then, in the face of their silence, Jesus launches into three parables. The first one is about two sons. The first son refuses to work in his father's vineyard but later changes his mind and heads to the vines. The second son says he will go work, but he doesn't. Jesus asks which man does his father's will. The leaders can't help but answer that it is the first, for, even though refusing at first, the man eventually goes to work. This first parable, like those that follow, is a warning about God's rejection of Israel's leadership—the chief priests, the scribes, the elders, and the rest. It is the "sinners and tax collectors" who, though rejecting God at first, now embrace Jesus and his inauguration of God's kingdom. Conversely, like the second son, the leaders claim to be leading the people to God but are actually leading them away, refusing to do the work of the kingdom brought to them by Jesus. Then Jesus launches right into another parable, often referred to as the Parable of the Wicked Tenants.

The Wicked Tenants

The context of this parable, falling in the midst of a direct confrontation between Jesus and the Jewish leaders, guides our interpretation of the parable. The landowner in the parable represents God and the vineyard represents God's people. Indeed, the parable's first verse is based directly on Isaiah 5, a song about an unfruitful vineyard (an unjust people). Thus, the "wicked tenants" are not the people themselves, but the leaders, both spiritual and political, who have repeatedly refused to understand God's

---

105.   The chief priests can't reply with "heaven" for that would be an endorsement of John and also Jesus. They can't answer "human," for John's movement was popular among the people. Jesus has a real gift for turning the tables on his accusers.

Law and God's work. Instead, the priests and pharisees exile his prophets and rebel against his Son.

When the landowner turns the vineyard over to new management, it is God opening his kingdom to those who embrace both God's work and God's son. It is a mistake to see this parable as speaking of God transferring the vineyard from the Jews to the Gentiles.[106] Rather, it is the Jewish leadership that is in Jesus' sight. Leadership of the vineyard is going to be given to a new crew, to those who will lead God's reconstituted people forward in a unity built on faith in Jesus Christ.

A Message for All

Jesus spoke this parable as a clear warning to those who had been leading Israel toward destruction rather than restoration. Jeremiah had confronted Israel's leaders and was imprisoned for it. Jesus' confrontation with them would lead him to a Roman cross only a few days later.

But it would be a mistake to hear this as a message only for the leaders. Had the Jews done what God had expected of them, loving God and neighbor? Had they embraced Jeremiah? They had welcomed Jesus on Sunday. Would they embrace him on Friday? Would the disciples themselves stand with him before the high priest, Caiaphas, or would they hide and even deny they knew him?

We face our own questions today as we strive to live in God's way and to see his work in the world. It can be hard to know what you have when you've got it, much less act on it. How good are we at discerning God's word today and heeding it? Do we strive to learn more so that we can be more discerning? Do we see the world through God-shaped glasses or "real world" glasses? Do we run our lives based on the world's priorities or upon God's? Do we stand up for the weak and oppressed, for those who can't stand up for themselves? Do we really appreciate all that God has given us, even in high-anxiety times? Questions such as these are not only for the "leaders," they are questions for us all.

Do we see what we have while we have it? God has given us the greatest gift imaginable, and we had better not miss it! What does Jesus ask of us? To

---

106. We should be mindful that the Jesus movement was a Jewish movement and would stay that way for several decades. It was more than ten years after Jesus' resurrection before a Gentile came to faith in Jesus Christ. None of the apostles, all of whom were Jewish, would have seen their embrace of Christ as leaving Judaism. They simply had come to embrace Jesus as Lord and as the Jewish Messiah.

jump in with both feet, to trust in him and to hope in him, to love others actively, and to lead like a servant—no less than that.

For a Deeper Understanding

The Hope of Israel

The vineyard was a common Hebrew metaphor for Israel; not so much the land, as the people. The people, Abraham's people, were the chosen of God, chosen for a purpose, to be the ones through whom God would rescue humanity and all the cosmos. Yet the people knew that they had not done well by God's vineyard, finding it impossible to simply love God and love neighbor every day and in every way. They saw the Babylonian exile as punishment for their sins, and the Roman soldiers were a daily reminder that they continued to live in a very real exile, despite having returned to the land.

Yet, in the midst of exile and alienation, prophets had brought powerful words of hope to the Jewish community in Babylon and after their return from exile. What were the dimensions of this hope?

Israel's hope was focused on the end of the exile which entailed three expectations: (1) liberation from oppression; (2) the restoration of the land; and (3) the rebuilding of the temple. All three expectations pointed toward the restoration of the people's relationship with the Lord God, to the forgiveness of Israel's sins, and to a new covenant.

It is easy to see why many would have thought that the exile was ending when Cyrus allowed the Jews to begin returning home. But as time went on, their hopes would be crushed. Yes, they were back on the land but it was occupied by foreigners. Indeed, the Jews were oppressed by one conqueror after another for centuries. Yes, they were allowed to rebuild the temple, but it was a pale reflection of the temple burned down by the Babylonians. As time passed, the Jews came to realize that the exile never really ended, that their sins had not been forgiven, that they still awaited their homecoming.

All this sets the stage for the parable, which tells the story of Israel's historic rejection of the prophets' call to return to God and, now, the violent unwillingness of the Jewish leadership to embrace Jesus as Messiah, the one who would usher in the long-awaited kingdom of God.

A Final Thought

I've written a lot of studies over the last two decades. I've been urged many times to pull some together in book form, but the project seemed awfully daunting, given everything that goes on at St. Andrew, the church where I serve on staff. But then Nancy Kurkowski, a regular class member, stepped forward and volunteered to take it on. She went through hundreds of studies and shaped some of them into this book, editing them, and making them work together. Without her faith, her dedication, and her skill, this book would never have come together. Here are her final thoughts on the book:

> **What does Jesus expect of us? To jump in with both feet and to pursue him with purpose; to trust him in all things and to hope in his word daily; to love others actively and not just talk about it; and to step up and lead like Jesus showed us. He expects no less than that.**
>
> **Nancy Kurkowski, August 2021**

I couldn't say it better myself . . . Scott